ADVENTURE TRAVEL WITH DOGS

PUPS ON PISTE

JACQUELINE MARY LAMBERT

Copyright & Disclaimer

© 2020 Jacqueline M. Lambert

All rights reserved. This book or any portion thereof may not be reproduced or used in any manner whatsoever without the express written permission of the author except for the use of brief quotations in a book review.

First Paperback Edition 2020

Book Cover Design and Formatting by Book Covers for You: www.bookcoversforyou.com

Map by Rocco Smeaton

The events and conversations in this book have been set down to the best of the author's ability, although some names and details may have been changed to protect the privacy of individuals.

All information, advice and tips in this book are based on the author's personal experience and do not constitute legal advice.

While every effort is made to ensure its veracity, there are no representations or warranties, express or implied, about the completeness, accuracy, reliability, suitability or availability with respect to the information, products or services contained in this book for any purpose. Any use of this information is at your own risk.

ISBN (paperback) 978-1-9993576-7-2

ISBN (ebook) 978-1-9993576-6-5

Contact:

Facebook:@JacquelineLambertAuthor

Amazon:www.amazon.com/author/jacquelinelambert

A Ski Season In Italy

Adventure Travel With Dogs

Pups on Piste

Jacqueline Lambert

By the Same Author

Adventure Caravanning with Dogs Series

- Year 1 – Fur Babies in France – *From Wage Slaves to Living the Dream*

- Dog on the Rhine – *From Rat Race to Road Trip*

- Dogs 'n' Dracula – *A Road Trip Through Romania*

Adventure Travel with Dogs Series

- Pups on Piste – *A Ski Season In Italy*

I would like to dedicate this book to my paternal aunts, June, Lilian and Anne, all of whom have been incredible role models for me. Long before it was common to do so, they each followed paths which defied the stereotypes of how girls were expected behave.

June Andrews – *a brilliant scientist with a great love of the outdoors. In an era when everyone left school in their early teens and, "there's no point educating girls", June won a grammar school scholarship and took it up, despite opposition. She studied science at technical college, because it was not on the school curriculum, then funded her degree by working full time, while helping out at home with her much younger siblings. She graduated from the University of London in Combined Maths and Science – and in doing so blazed a trail that meant if they wished, her sisters could not be denied an education or career.*

Lilian Dinsdale – *who has climbed, trekked and skied her way around Europe. Schoolchildren in Lancashire might remember her as 'The Skiing Nurse', who accompanied them on many school trips.*

Anne Thomas – *a horse-loving, sailing and windsurfing*

instructor with a passion for travel and biology, who has had a profound impact on many young lives. On a family holiday, Anne was responsible for initiating both Mark's and my compulsive obsession with windsurfing.

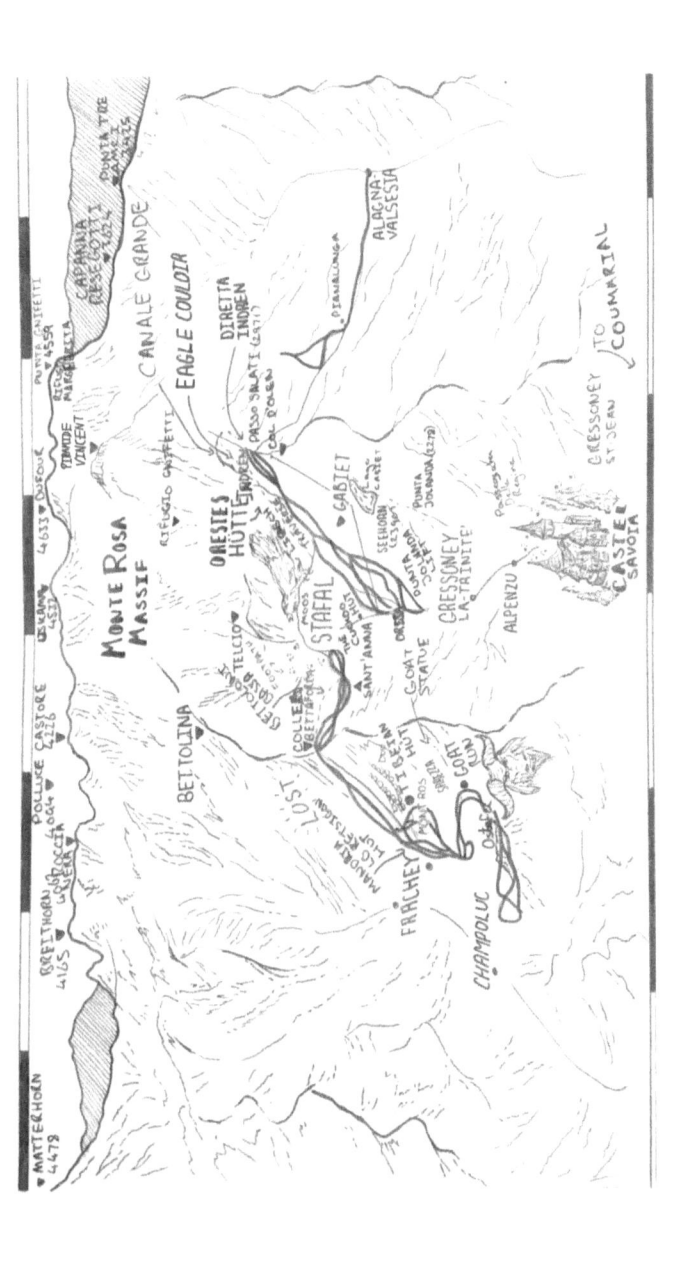

PROLOGUE

A Dream Descent – Heliski on the Marmolada Glacier, Dolomites, Italy

On Edges, Sidecut & Why "It's Not Steep if you can Turn!"

"I want to have his babies!"

This might seem a strange thing to say to your husband about your ski instructor after a private lesson, but two hours with Mario changed my life. In skiing terms, at least, the wife that Mark reclaimed following an afternoon with Super Mario was barely recognisable.

We were staying in Arabba – not the easiest resort for a beginner; certainly not a nervous beginner whose skiing confidence had been shattered by a serious injury on her second ever ski trip.

Our hotel was ski-in, ski-out – a steep and difficult black run brought you 'in'. 'Out' was off-piste, and involved a rough traverse followed by a bumpy descent to the lift. Of course, the un-groomed traverse could also be 'in' if you didn't fancy tackling the black. Hobson's third choice was a lengthy, treacherous walk up and down a narrow, icy road in slippery ski boots, carrying skis.

A group decision had been made to ski the Marmolada Glacier. Our rep said that, from Monte Cherz, a €20-per-head helicopter trip would whisk us up to the summit before the lifts opened.

The 12km long *Bellunese* from the top of Marmolada to Malga Ciapella is the longest slope in the Dolomites. It has a vertical drop of 1,823m and in 1935, hosted the world's first slalom ski race; the *Gigantissimo della Marmolada*.

La Pista Bellunese is a groomed and marked red run, with a short, black option at one point. It is not considered difficult, but the knowledge that I was the weakest link within the group haunted me. For the whole week, an unspoken question hung over us all: a cloud of doubt regarding my confidence and ability to join the trip.

The previous day, I had cried on a blue run. In most resorts, including Arabba, blue is for beginners; the lowest designation of difficulty. My chances of tackling the Marmolada had never seemed so remote. So, when I skidded into a parallel hockey stop and sprayed a little shower of snow over Mark, he was aghast.

"What on earth has happened to you?!" he asked.

The new, skiing me grinned back at him, brimming with newly-discovered assurance.

I have often praised the fact that I am part of the carbon fibre generation. My aunt, Lilian, skied all her life in leather boots, strapped to long, straight wooden skis that weighed a ton. In the 1990s, a revolution occurred in two of my favourite sports; windsurfing and skiing. It was a transformation in both concept and construction, with huge technological advances expedited by the invention of new strong but lightweight compounds.

Long, straight windsurf boards got shorter, wider and more stable. They adopted a curved rocker shape, which made them more manoeuvrable. At the same time, skis evolved from lengthy planks with parallel edges to the shorter, waisted carving, 'shaped' or 'parabolic' skis that almost everyone rides today. These two simple innovations opened up both sports. With modern materials and more forgiving designs, learning and progress became quicker and easier overnight.

Travelling over snow on lengths of wood is not a new concept. Stone Age cave paintings from 8,000 B.C, in Altai, China, show ancient hunters gliding along on something that resembles skis. The world's oldest relic of a ski, found near Lake Sindor in Russia, dates back to around 6,300 B.C.

Although its popularity grew in the 1990s, shaping

the edge of skis with 'sidecut' is also not a new idea. In the early 1800s, craftsmen in Telemark, Norway, knew that carving the waist of their wooden skis into an hourglass-shape made them easier to turn. In 1926, Rudolf Lettner, an Austrian accountant, invented steel edges for skis after almost falling to his death down an icy slope, because his wooden ski edges wouldn't grip.

On a flat piece of snow at the top of the lift, Mario introduced me to these concepts,

"Let me show you what these skis can do. Just put them on their side and they turn."

As he set off slowly, he flexed his ankles to lay his skis on their edges and carved a long arc across the snow. As I tried it, the metal edges of my ski dug in and gripped; I felt like I was on tracks. I realised that making a turn on carving skis was effortless.

Mario took me to Bec de Roces and forced me ski down my nemesis; the steeper and narrower of the two red runs. I scooted across the top of the slope, shopping for turns. You know the deal,

"I'll turn in a minute; in a minute... Ooh. I can't turn now. I'm right at the edge!"

I came to rest facing the side of the piste, with no room to carve another arc. My pre-Mario recovery strategy would have involved seating myself comfortably on the snow, before performing a half roll to face my skis the opposite way. Then, I might have stood up to ski on or, if it was steep and my confidence was low, I might slide down the edge of the slope on my backside to lose height. Mario was horrified.

"Just stand upright on your skis and they will float away down the hill."

To my surprise, it worked.

In two hours, I learned to start, stop and change direction in complete control. That was all I needed to know. Since then, the mantra, "It's not steep if you can turn," has served me well.

"Do you think I'll be able to ski the Marmolada tomorrow?" I asked at the end of the lesson.

Mario's parting shot as I sprayed my little shower of snow over Mark was, "You – you can ski *anything*!"

The following morning started with a heart-in-the-mouth race over to Monte Cherz to catch our helicopter at 9am. First in the queue as the lifts opened at 8.30am, we chased like hooligans down two pistes and caught three lifts to get there. As we boarded, blown snow from the rotors exfoliated our faces like a sandstorm.

Most of the group had never flown in a helicopter. I used to fly light aircraft and once had a helicopter lesson. On that day, a Robinson R-22 two-seater shot straight to the top of my shopping list, should I ever win the Lottery. A helicopter's extraordinary ability to stop dead and hover in mid-air, or make a sudden, sharp, vertical rise was an airborne thrill equivalent to aerobatics.

Our pilot demonstrated this to perfection by

aiming straight for the jagged ridges that lay between us and Marmolada, before pulling up vertically to miss the crags by inches. We flew over Porto Vescovo and the frozen Lake Fedaia, before climbing to Punta Rocca at 3,269m. Marmolada is the highest mountain in the Dolomites. Dwarfed by the scale of the landscape, our puny, little craft seemed too fragile to survive. As it wobbled down to land on the knife-edge ridge in a howling gale, we were all too aware of the dizzy swoop just ahead, which dropped thousands of feet straight down to the valley below.

As we disembarked, we were assaulted by both the tempest and the downdraft from the rotors. We grabbed our skis from the box on the side of the 'copter and rushed through the maelstrom to safety as best we could. Our priorities were to get out of the scouring, icy wind and away from the precipice as quickly as possible. The pilot's priority seemed to be to get away. I am still surprised that a helicopter could fly in such strong winds. Once he rose shakily back aloft, like one of the models in *Thunderbirds*, we felt abandoned and isolated; left alone to court the terrifying majesty of Marmolada, 'The Queen of the Dolomites' – and whatever she chose to throw at us.

The wind that had closed the gondola groaned and whistled through the cables. As a group, we hastily sought shelter in the lift station, which was eerie and deserted. A flurry of snow followed us in, whirling like a powdery Dervish before collapsing on the threshold as the gale slammed the door behind us. Like the fists of a thwarted giant trying to get in, angry air battered the outside of the building. Otherwise, the interior was calm and silent, with a 1950s atmosphere that smelled of oil, yellowed paint and *Bakelite*. We felt trapped, as though awaiting our fate in Ice Station Zebra.

Six pale, scared faces regarded each other, knowing that at some point, we had to forsake the warmth and shelter and take on the blizzard. Our location literally took our breath away. At over 10,000ft, we had thirty percent less oxygen than at sea level.

When we did finally make our move, we had the entire, glacial wilderness to ourselves. We carved steep swathes through drifted powder-snow interspersed with bands of golden rock. From Malga Ciapella in the valley, Punta Rocca, is accessed by three successive cable cars. The altitude of the initial piste from the summit is usually enough to guarantee beautiful snow. Nevertheless, no subsequent visit to The Queen has compared to the shin-deep, virgin powder that she granted for our first ever run.

By the time we reached Sass del Mul, the start of the Punta Rocca cable car, the wind had dropped. At nearly 3,000m on the Serauta ridge, there is an interesting WWI museum inside the lift station. However, we opted to re-ascend as quickly as possible, to score a second descent before the crowds from Malga Ciapella caught us up. Our re-run of the floury powder was lovely, but a few other intrepid souls, who interrupted the flow and encroached upon our splendid isolation, disturbed the solitude.

We elected to return to Arabba via Passo Padon and took the chairlift just beyond the Rifugio Fedaia. Had we followed the shallow slopes into Malga Ciapella, we would have been forced to queue for the three cable cars and go back to the top of Marmolada. Our burning thighs rebelled at the thought of reprising *La Bellunese*.

My experience of skiing has never been the same since. This was a mind-boggling, eye-opener on the breadth and immensity of the thrill that sliding down the side of a mountain can offer. It is also something that I would never have experienced had it not been for Mario.

And that, dear reader, is why I wanted to have his babies!

1

THE ITALIAN JOB

"You don't look old enough to have given up work!" The start of our season in Monte Rosa.

Scroll back to the 9th January 1999. I was newly single. The first step of my comeback into polite society was forcing myself to attend a late New Year party. As I walked into the function room alone, I took a deep breath. A very tall man was leaning against the bar. "He's handsome!" I thought, but it didn't occur to me that within thirty-seven days, we would be engaged. I certainly didn't expect to be married to him thirty-seven weeks later.

Subsequently, the organiser explained to me why she had chosen to seat us together for dinner, "I thought you'd get on."

Within a single conversation, the man and I realised that most of our desires and ambitions were the same. A major one was a shared passion for planks and an impossible dream; to spend a full season on the snow.

Almost two decades on, I could not have foreseen how Mark and I would spend the anniversary of our meeting. The 9th of January was the first day of our three-month stay in a ski apartment in beautiful Monte Rosa, Italy.

2,000 metres above sea level, water boils at 93°C.

"What's that got to do with anything?" you might ask, but these things matter.

Your cup of tea won't brew properly for a start. And if you want to soft boil an egg up a mountain, it takes seven minutes, not four. High altitude cooking; chalet hosting; food safety – we'd been preparing ourselves to get more snow time. We'd lodged our C.V.s with *Natives,* had an interview with *Collett's* and hobnobbed our way around the ski show at Olympia. However, jointly, in our wildest dreams, we had never envisaged that we would achieve our fantasy without working.

"You don't look old enough to have given up work!"

Everyone tells us this. We obviously don't look wealthy either (and we're not!) – so how did we do it?

Our answer is simple; we got tenants in. The rental income from our house covers costs and bills for a basic apartment in a small, uncrowded Italian ski resort. There is even a little left over to spend – so we earn money by doing it. Of course, we had to render ourselves homeless – and that is the point at which every bloke we've ever met absolves himself by saying,

"I'd do it like a shot – but the wife won't go for it!"

Made redundant in our early fifties, the lightbulb moment came when we accidentally bought a caravan. We named her 'Kismet', which means 'destiny' or 'fate', and got a bit giddy following a few drinks to celebrate.

"We could rent out the house and move into the caravan. It would be a really cheap way to live!"

As sobriety and the grey light of dawn allowed reality to permeate back into our consciousness, we realised that it was a tremendous idea. So, we had been living in Kismet since June. Although we spent the summer touring France, which was fabulous, our return to Britain in the autumn hadn't always felt like Livin' the Dream.

New Year's Day brought another grey dawn. An interval between bottle and throttle seemed wise, so it was late afternoon before we left our friends' house in Dorset to drive to Sussex. There, we collected Kismet from storage and, in the pouring rain, drove her to Surrey to spend some time with Mark's family. When we arrived, we had to pitch in the wet, freezing cold and dark.

Imagine the joy when we opened the caravan door to find Kismet's interior flooded for the second time. Our brand-new carpets, replaced after the last flood, were saturated. On the plus side, our van, Big Blue, wasn't bogged down in mud and our cameras and important documents were not floating around in Kismet's lockers. This was a significant improvement on the last occasion. I suppose that sometimes, you have just got to count your blessings, but it was not the greatest start to the New Year.

"You make caravanning sound so appealing..." our friend Stefano empathised when we regaled him with our most recent mobile misfortune. Recalling the joys of camping reminded me of a newbie friend who had marvelled at the size of the campsite toilet that he had visited during the night,

"It was the size of a bath. I nearly fell in!"

He'd found the septic waste disposal.

A few hardy souls do opt to ski from mobile homes, albeit usually for a week or two, rather than a season. We specified Kismet carefully to enable us to survive year-round occupation – and potential trips to the Alps. A *Bailey Unicorn Vigo*, she has state-of-the-art insulation and a highly efficient *Alde* heating system. Other than when the heating fluid was depleted because, following a service, the dealer cross threaded the tank closure and it leaked all over Mark's clothes, we have never had a chilly night in Kismet.

Our decision to over-winter 'in the brick' was mostly down to moisture. The prospect of trying to dry four wet dogs and two wet skiers in a caravan did not appeal. In any case, the cost of our seasonal rental was similar to site fees, it was conveniently located near the ski lifts, rather than an unconnected village down the valley – and it didn't require us to tow a seven-metre leviathan up icy hairpins.

Amid a frantic bout of pre-departure visits to friends and family, we packed our trusty Hyundai iLoad van, Big Blue, for three months away. Big Blue takes her name from the ocean, 'The Big Blue' – highly appropriate for a vehicle often filled with windsurfing equipment, although her cargo this time was a little different.

"We don't need to worry about capacity!"

As when we departed for the summer, these were Mark's famous last words, once again.

Later, he warned me, "Be careful if you open any of the van doors..."

Had Big Blue been offered a wafer-thin mint in a *Monty Python* film, there is no doubt that she would have uttered an expletive, then exploded.

And so, our three-month trip to Monte Rosa in the Italian Alps began with a long day of driving; from Surrey back to Sussex to store our beloved Kismet, before making our way to a dog-friendly seafront hotel in Folkstone, near The Channel Tunnel for our crossing. We had no time to deal with Kismet's moisture problem. Following the previous flood, our dealer had given Kismet a clean bill of health and stated that it was, "A one off." Since the flooding only happened when she was towed in the rain, we had to trust that in storage, she would be fine.

It was The Hounds' first stay in a hotel and they each reacted differently. Nosy Rosie, our black and white girl, went for a good explore, while Kai and Ruby took advantage of the facilities to hand and languished on the bed (Princess Ruby the Red stole prime position on the pillow). Lani was quick to observe that starched, white bed linen and rolled, white towels were a perfect foil on which to rub her little, black, fish face, garnered from our pre-check-in walk on the beach.

Four dogs attracted plenty of attention as we ate dinner in front of a crackling, log fire. Leaving their husbands swearing loudly at the bar, two ladies came over to pet the pups. They fired out the usual questions,

"What breed are they?"

"Cavapoos."

"Have-a-poos? *HA HA HA HA HA!* What's that?"

"Cavalier King Charles Spaniel crossed with a Poodle."

"Are they related?"

"No. They're all the same age, but from different families."

"Why do you have four dogs?"

"We were getting two, but didn't quite stop…"

Then the conversation drifted to the reason we were in the hotel.

"You're skiing in Italy for three months? You don't look old enough to have given up work!"

The following day started as it should for those who depart the fair shores of Blighty; Stephen with a stiffy – a Fry up. Our National Treasure's twig 'n' berries were followed by a bracing walk on a grey beach and a very kind man in *Halfords* allaying a last-minute panic by checking Big Blue's antifreeze levels.

"You'll be OK unless you're going to the Arctic, mate!" he assured Mark. He didn't charge – and we even got free coffee and a biscuit for his trouble.

Heading *Eurotunnel*-wards, we felt fully prepared for a Continental Alpine Climate on our difficult-to-source winter van tyres. They had eventually been delivered from Berlin. Our cooling system was now replete with ethylene glycol from *Halfords* and we had,

"A lot of tinned food. We're going skiing for three months."

This was in reply to Martin, who X-rayed Big Blue at customs.

"You don't look old enough to have given up work," he told us.

The headline in the local paper at our interim stopover needed no translation, *'Froid Sibérien dans le Haut Jura; -18°C à Saint Pierre!'*

A Siberian cold snap provided us with good reason to self-congratulate on our winter driving preparations. It was also during this part of our trip that we had our first experience of the phenomenon known as 'The Paw.'

Our little, black girl, Lani, suddenly discovered that she requires chest and tummy tickles at all times while travelling. Stop tickling her tummy, even for a few seconds to attend to your own needs (such as scratching your nose – or trying to regain feeling in your tummy tickling hand) and 'The Paw' launches instantly into action.

'The Paw' is an impatient series of sharp and insistent scratches, which continue until satisfactory tummy tickling is resumed. Like a qualified acupuncturist, 'The Paw' is very particular about the location of tickling points. Get it wrong and you can be sure that as Lani sits impassive, 'The Paw' will be there to correct you, shoving your hand roughly to a more acceptable position. It seemed that the owner of 'The Paw' had experienced an epiphany. At last, she had worked out why she got a human as a pet.

Our return to France felt like a homecoming; I had missed her. Once, I had rebelled against all things French; the awful exports that they foisted on us, like Golden Delicious apples, *Le Piat D'Or* and William the Conqueror. Napoleon called the British "a nation of shopkeepers", but they killed Oscar Wilde with wallpaper and started the Franco-Prussian war because they objected to the wording of the Ems Telegram. *(In a run-down Parisian hotel, the reputed last words of Oscar Wilde were, "My wallpaper and I are fighting a duel to the death. One or other of us has got to go.")*

When I analysed it, my actual experience of France did not justify this prejudice. Other than one rude waiter in Paris, which is to be expected, perhaps even desired, France and the French had treated me to nothing but kindness over the years. Possibly, I harboured a hidden resentment for their thirty-five-hour working week and months of annual leave, which they top up regularly with strikes.

Over our three-month trip in the summer, *La Belle France* had truly captivated me. The uncrowded roads; the magical scenery; and the sense of freedom that comes from having a whole continent just down the road. It all made me glad to have left behind our cramped and stressful isle.

A *Hotel Ibis Budget* provided our stopover in Dole. After scouting the local area, which consisted exclusively of 'industrial estate', we decided that our best option for dinner was a ready meal for two, dispensed from a machine in the foyer. We know how to roll on a Saturday night, we who are Livin' the Dream!

Froid Sibérien? I can't be certain, but it snowed enough overnight for a collective wonder about where in the packed-to-the-gunwales van we might find the windscreen scraper. A credit card was co-opted to de-ice our screen, then we tested our brakes in the slippery car park. We praised the grip of our new winter tyres, before striking forth in the exact opposite direction to the Mont Blanc tunnel.

Once we did a U-Turn and started moving the right way, Mont Blanc-wards, we wound through the beautiful scenery of the Haut Jura. On the familiar carriageway of the Autoroute Blanche, we encountered a double paradox; we got stuck behind a *cautious* Italian driver – *in a BMW*!

C'mon. Italians have a reputation for reckless motoring machismo to uphold – and the BMW is the stereotypical vehicle of the inconsiderate lunatic. What's your luck?

In most circumstances, our prudent paradox would have presented no real concern. After towing a caravan for six months, we had lost any need for speed. However, along with a maximum speed limit of 70kph, the Mont Blanc tunnel also has a *minimum* speed limit of 50kph. Thankfully, we received no fines for fandangling as we trailed in the wake of our Latin laggard.

Pizza Side, as we crawled from the gloom of the tunnel into blinding sunshine, he pulled over. As we drove down the Aosta valley, streams of Italians shot past us, shattering the speed limit by a factor of at least two. This restored our confidence in Italian motoring skills, but was extremely unnerving, since the *autostrada* passes through a succession of tunnels. A fire in there and you'd never get out alive; but crashing and burning is as nothing to maintaining the manly pride of a *guidatore*.

It was still daylight when we arrived in Staffal. This was a blessing, because although I say 'arrived', we actually got stuck about two feet shy of our final destination. Stymied by a slight incline, topped by a petite mound of snow and ice at the entrance to the garage, it took us a further hour and a half to propel Big Blue those final few centimetres over the threshold. Our 1,000-mile epic had ended slightly short, especially in metric, and caused Mark to launch into full-scale rhetorical exasperation.

"You mean I need to put on the freakin' snow chains for the last eighteen inches of the journey?!"

The answer was, "Yes" – and they broke.

The snow chain is a curious piece of equipment with its own, special air of mystery. Snow chains like to be coaxed and cajoled around a wheel by a supplicant, who is forced to kneel in the snow. Too fiddly for gloves, they extend no empathy to fingers that fluff and fumble due to loss of feeling or the onset of frostbite. They afford no quarter for those forced to fiddle beneath a wheel arch, frozen and smutty with salt and slush. Once on, your snow chain requires a gentle seduction and persuasion to encourage it to grip. Spinning rapidly on sheet ice is not acceptable to a snow chain. Snow chains thus abused will express their disdain in a variety of ways; from the simple mutiny of a violent snap, to wrapping around your axle in an intricate and inextricable, steely embrace.

Our almost instantaneous loss of the snow chains was devastating. The main weapon in our anti-skid arsenal, this forced us into all kinds of desperate measures: hammering ice out from under Big Blue's wheels and using gripper treads, which turned into high-energy ballistic missiles when rotated upon by a wheel on ice. In the end, a decisive shove from a passing group of burly Swedes in ski boots thrust Big Blue's drive wheels on to concrete. From there, friction restored traction and we finally completed the last few inches of our journey.

The welcome from our hostess, Sylvia, was as warm as the brilliant Italian sunshine. She was a little surprised when she saw the volume of personal effects that disgorged from Big Blue. We didn't have the kitchen sink, but we did have a super-king-size memory foam mattress and rather a lot of corned beef, as well as all our pots, pans and the travelling *Wedgewood* dinner service.

The *Wedgewood* had been pressed into action when our entire set of everyday crockery had fallen out of the back of Big Blue on Tuckton Roundabout in Bournemouth. It seemed silly to replace it when our 'best' china had languished unused in the back of a cupboard for decades. In essence, we had emptied Kismet of everyday essentials and brought it all along. Prior experience of Continental self-catering equipage prompted us to preventative measures against dubiously hygienic wooden spoons and pans which add lumps of *Teflon* or rust to your food. We knew that we could expect an espresso maker but no kettle, that all the cups would be the size of thimbles – and the potential for finding a sharp knife or potato peeler was zero.

A previous one-week stay in the residence B.C. (Before Canines) had also alerted us to the discomfort afforded by its small sofa bed, even without four pups in tow. Trying to buy food in resort was another trap that we would not fall into again. The worst meal that I have ever eaten was one that I cooked myself. It was a *Ready, Steady, Cook*-type challenge, using the supplies available from the telephone box that passes for the local shop in Staffal. The potatoes on offer were green and wizened. We turned them down in favour of the best selection from the few items that appeared fit for human consumption. In the end, our gourmet experience comprised a sausage, which could not have looked more like a turd if it tried, accompanied by a rubbery cauliflower, sulphurous with decay, sporting a sweaty crown of molten, mousetrap cheese.

Multi-functionality is our key to packing light. Mark is a whizz at configuring small spaces. In the apartment, he moved the furniture around and constructed a bed base for the super-king-size memory foam mattress from our plastic storage boxes. These had served the dual function of containers to transport the tonnage of corned beef and P.G. Tips required to sustain us for a three month stay in Italy. When Sylvia came in to discuss puppy-sitting, she marvelled at how our rearranged room looked much bigger, despite the addition of a super-king-size bed.

By the process of direct experimentation, (i.e. he stood on one) Mark discovered that the lid of a single plastic box could not support his 100kg body weight. A swift assessment of the damage revealed that it was B.B.D.T. – Broken Beyond Duct Tape.

Italy is a culture where shops selling designer skiwear are universal, even in our miniscule village, whose food shop didn't stock an edible potato. In Monte Rosa, the ski instructors are clad in *Emporio Armani*. However, unlike the U.K., the high streets are devoid of useful shops; like a vast array of outlets offering a tempting cornucopia of differently-sized plastic boxes for £1 each. As such, we had no choice but *Jugaad* – a Hindi-Urdu colloquialism, which roughly translates as 'an innovative fix' or 'hack'.

In a stroke of absolute genius, Mark fixed the bed. He turned the box upside down.

Exhausted by our three-day, 1,000-mile epic, we collapsed on to our improvised, super-king-size memory foam crib. We had driven for nearly twenty-four hours (for twenty-three of which Lani was demanding tummy tickles) and had undertaken two tunnel-tastic crossings; 150-feet under the sea floor of the English Channel and then beneath a 4,810m peak.

We had lugged our shopping from the supermarket in Aosta up the stairs from the garage to our room, along with a plenitude of household items, and fifteen tonnes of corned beef.

With Big Blue so full, the only remaining space to pack our haul from the bottom-of-the-mountain supermarket sweep was the dog bed. For hygiene reasons, I had intended to cook the packet of mince, sampled en route by a Mystery Muncher, strongly suspected to be Ruby. However, we were beside ourselves with fatigue and the best I could manage for dinner was a tin of pea and ham soup.

A bottle of local wine seemed a fitting way to celebrate our arrival. It was a *Torrette Superior*. What can I say? The spelling is *slightly* different, but it still made us snigger and think of the sweary chaps at the bar back in Folkstone.

It was f***** nice. B******.

2

PUPS ON PISTE

The Mystery Muncher Strikes Again; A Day of New Experiences & Pathetic Pup Cam

Like so many fantastic discoveries, we happened upon Monte Rosa by accident. A last-minute, birthday ski trip to a quiet and little-known Italian resort took us to Staffal, a tiny hamlet just above Gressoney la Trinité, in the Valle del Lys.

Ninety minutes from Turin and two hours from Milan, many of the apartments in the valley are holiday homes. This means that, other than weekends and major holidays, it is like having your own, personal ski resort.

People moaned about Staffal in reviews on the internet;

"It only has three bars!"

"It was really quiet!"

Had we wanted Après Ski, we would have gone to

Austria. 'Quiet' made us think, "Fantastic!", so we booked it immediately. It was the start of a long and lasting love affair.

One of the ski areas of the Aosta Valley, which runs east from the Mont Blanc tunnel, Monte Rosa is Italy's 'Three Valleys'. Nestling beneath the Monte Rosa Massif, home to the second highest summit in the Alps and Western Europe, the surrounding 4,000m peaks include the Matterhorn. *Cervino* as she is known in these parts, is Europe's 'third mountain' in terms of altitude.

On piste, Monte Rosa is a small but perfectly formed ski resort. The pistes run between the three main resort villages of Champoluc, Gressoney and Alagna; one in each valley. This means you can go places, rather than just taking a lift up and skiing down the same mountain. Staffal is central and well-connected, with modern lifts from the village centre to both of the other valleys. If you ski from top to bottom, there are also some delightfully long descents. For example, Passo Salati to Alagna is 8km long with a 1,768m difference in elevation.

Monte Rosa is an intermediate resort. The piste map looks like a blood circulation diagram – all red. Apart from nursery slopes and a couple of small collections of blue runs, high on the mountain and accessible by gondola, there is very little really easy skiing. However, the black runs are not particularly difficult either and being Italy, everything is groomed to perfection every night.

The big surprise for such a mini resort is the extent of its off-piste paradise. Monte Rosa has cult status for freeride skiing. I read that it is one of the 'Top 5 Off-Piste Destinations in the World'. It was named 'No. 1 in Europe' by *Powderhounds* and 'The Alps' Best Kept Secret' by *Fall Line Magazine.*

Polvere Rosa – Pink Powder, is a book an inch thick, which details many of the off-piste routes in the area. The Punta Indren lift serves only off-piste itineraries and Alagna dubs itself 'Alagna Freeride Paradise'. There are also extensive glacier heliskiing opportunities, including an international trip from Monte Rosa to Zermatt in Switzerland.

Unfortunately, following our journey of a thousand miles, we awoke feeling as though we had been used for trampolining practice by The Big Mommas and their herd of bouncing, baby elephants. Although it was a beautiful, bluebird day and a paradise of wintry bliss lay outside our front door, neither of us felt anything like skiing.

With no new snow for some time, the conditions were icy and hard-packed. On previous, one-week skiing holidays, we would queue for the first lift and not return until dark. We would allow ourselves a maximum twenty-minute break for lunch and, according to our G.P.S., skied an average of fifty miles per day. "Too far; too long; too fast" were the criticisms levelled at us when unsuspecting friends elected to ski, walk or cycle with us. It was this kind of torture that led to our being christened *The Bastard Lamberts.*

It was a relief not to feel that we had to spend every waking moment on the slopes. We wanted to make sure that we had settled the dogs in the apartment before we left them and after all, we had three months. There would be snow. Sometime. And we would ski. Sometime!

In the back of my mind, however, I couldn't help thinking, "Is this going to be a repeat of our road trip in the summer that didn't go anywhere...?"

Our first winter walk took us up a grassy track on which we had once skied off-piste. The pups had never experienced snow, so we were delighted that they loved it. Watching them play and chase each other around was an absolute joy. Lani, Ruby and Rosie seemed to enjoy eating ice and everybody joined in with the fun of bounding after snowballs. When we reached the edge of the black run, Moos, we took our inaugural picture of the Pups on Piste. To Mark's chagrin, it would be the first photo of many.

With a coffee on our terrace, we watched the setting sun blush and paint the mountains pink. It might seem a fitting colour for Monte Rosa, although sources suggest that the name derives from a local patois word *rouése,* meaning 'glacier'; rather than *rosa,* the Italian for 'pink'.

The Fab Four did a few walls of death around the building before going to play in a pile of snow at the back. They seemed to love Monte Rosa as much we did. We felt immediately relaxed and excited to have arrived. And snow was forecast.

The Mystery Muncher struck again. Not satisfied with quietly nibbling away at the pack of minced beef on the way up from the supermarket in Aosta, the zip of my fleece jacket started to shed teeth. Note to Self; keep both shopping *and* outdoor clothing out of reach of canines – particularly one Princess Ruby.

The following day, we applied *Mushers' Secret Paw Protector Wax* to protect the pups' paddy paws from winter hazards and help with grip. On the tiled floor of the apartment, the results were hilarious. All that was missing was a background rendition of *Bolero* as The Fab Four slid around like Olympic Figure-Skating Legends, Torvill and Dean.

The day continued to evolve into an epoch of new experiences – both for us and our Continental Cavapoos. After parting with €1,600 for two seasonal lift passes, we discovered that we could have saved €100 each if we'd bought them before November. To get our money's worth, we all boarded the Gabiet gondola and headed up into mountains.

Monte Rosa prides itself on being dog-friendly. Dogs are welcome in many mountain huts, as well as on cable cars, gondolas and *Navetta* shuttle buses. They should wear a muzzle on the buses and cable cars, although being Italy, it is not always enforced.

Kai and Ruby took the ascent completely in their stride. Usually the bravest, Rosie was slightly reluctant to board the gondola. Poor little Lani, who is not a fan of escalators and most modes of transport other than

Big Blue, was trembling and needed a cuddle all the way up.

Everyone recovered their composure in the blue and white glory that greeted us at 2,300m. As we crunched through fresh snow, Mark and I were forced to recover our *YakTrax* snow-chains-for-shoes every couple of steps. We overcame this eventually by tying a shoe lace to each side of the *YakTrax* and passing it over the top of our boots to keep them on. (*YakTrax* has now adopted our brilliant innovation, although their Velcro strap is slightly smarter than our shoe lace solution.)

The Pawsome Foursome proved a hit when we stopped for refreshments in the *Adler Nest – The Eagle's Nest* mountain hut. Several ski groups insisted on taking selfies with them, however I was denied photographic satisfaction. Our travels seem blighted by problems with technology. We packed light on the camera front. I mean, how many cameras do you need when you travel with a photo-phobic husband? The answer is more than one if the battery in your only camera discharges every five minutes. It looked like a repeat of the laptop battery debacle, whose replacement had posed such a riddle as we toured rural France during the summer.

I said it was a day of new experiences and for the first time, we took the dogs with us to the tiny gym in the basement of our apartment block. A Cavapoo emulating my standing stretches by rearing up on his hind legs certainly made my workout much less of a chore. Conditioning my abs with Ruby curled up on my shoulder was even moderately enjoyable.

Still, those of us who are Livin' the Dream do have mundane things to contend with – and that includes laundry. Perhaps the most exciting thing that happened all day was the inauguration of our new, portable washing machine. Against launderette fees, we had calculated a four-week return on investment for this mean mutha.

To our horror, we realised that its instructions were in the front drawer of the caravan, back in Selsey, although I could boast some experience with twin-tubs from my student days. I guess it's like riding a bike – or milking a goat as I did in June for the first time in thirty years. You can't explain how to do it, but the muscle memory remains. Anyhow, the instruction manual was probably written in 'English As She Is Spoke.' I can't tell you how satisfying it was to get it working.

Mark passed his twin-tub apprenticeship with flying colours; he managed to cleanse that most exacting of loads – a super-king-size duvet cover. Paradoxically, the portable washing machine, besides saving us money, allows us to travel light, since we need fewer clothes.

We also instigated a rule that our few remaining possessions should be as multi-functional as possible. The washing machine fitted this requirement perfectly; doubling as both a laundry basket and a dog barrier when placed in front of the open patio door.

But for me, the best thing about it was that Mark loved using it. I would never need to do laundry again!

Alpine hosts feel obliged to maintain room temperatures at a level which could smelt steel. It was -20°C outside and snowing. We turned down the heating – but still had to sleep with the windows open.

Our excitement built as we collected our newly edged and waxed skis from Ezio, Carlos and Simone in the local ski shop *Ambaradanspitz*, whose advertising hoarding proposes the unforgettable combination of *Lamine e Birra – Ski Edges & Beer.*

Would today be the day we finally christened the planks?

That would be a 'No!' We stayed with the pups for *just one more day* to make sure that they felt settled and secure in the apartment. You must understand that we get separation anxiety if we're apart from our fur babies.

On Mark's birthday, we decided that we had to ski. My brother was amused by the email that we sent him that morning.

"Our wills and all the doggie details are in the black folder in our apartment. If we die a freezing death on the slopes, can you repatriate our pups?"

"It's always good to contemplate mortality on your birthday!" he replied.

We left Die Hunde home alone for two whole

hours. Not because that's as long as they can be left, but because that's as long as we could bear to be without them. After a two-year snow drought, you would think the most important point was; could we remember how to ski? However, for me, the more pertinent question was; did our ski pants still fit?

It was so unfair. Despite Mark supplementing his diet with copious amounts of cake, chocolate and biscuits, his salopettes slid down to his ankles, while my new, pink powder pants had, er, shrunk… I would need be more diligent with that gym business if I wished to maintain a dry derrière during our back-country ski course in a couple of weeks.

When we did get on to Monte Rosa's slopes, they were characteristically crowded; what, with both Mark *and* I cluttering them up.

Sylvia had promised to keep an eye on our pooches, although as an extra precaution to make sure that they were fine, we left a camera to monitor them. Unfortunately, 'Pup Cam' was set on 'still' – taking a photo every three seconds – rather than 'video'. The result was 4,800 photographs of a sofa bed draped with a purple blanket – which left us absolutely none the wiser as to what the pups got up to while we were out.

3

WINTER WALKIES – FOOTPATH NO. 7: TO THE SOURCE OF THE LYS

Cavapoos, Couloirs & The Sad Story of Mimma & Guido

Footpath No. 7 is not a romantic name for the narrow path that passes beneath Punta Telcio on its winding way from Staffal towards the Monte Rosa Massif. Follow it all the way, and you will find the source of the River Lys.

The route passes by a stone cattle shed from where, if you pause, you see a deep canyon to your left. Sliced by water through the bedrock over millennia, here, the upper Lys changes character. She becomes narrow and wild, tumbling down drops and echoing her passing within the natural amphitheatre of sheer, vertical cliffs.

On your right, a large boulder bears a plaque. If you look up the steep, rock walls of Telcio's western face, a narrow couloir draws your gaze. In Italian, the plaque reads; *'In memory of Mimma and Guido, who were swept away by the avalanche here, on December 7, 1987.'*

They had been unfortunate; we felt incredibly sad for them, but didn't think that their accident had anything to do with us. We formed up The Fab Four on the snow for a Puppy Pose and photographed Cavapoos and a Couloir.

For those who observe closely, the mountains are filled with memorial plaques, votive pillars, crosses and small, white chapels, which are hundreds of years old. The Walser people who inhabited this uncompromising environment were both superstitious and deeply religious. Although these symbols are a form of worship, they were also placed to act as protection – and as a warning. Experienced mountain folk may respect the dangers, but even they sometimes get caught out.

The early part of the ascent is towards a white, gabled house on the hillside, which forms part of the summer hamlet of Cortalys. Here, a few streams bicker down the mountainside to join the Lys. Where they cross the path, they provide a useful refreshment pit-stop for puppies.

Opposite the white house, we clambered up on to a knoll and peered down into the Lys canyon. Wary of the cliff, I had my photo taken on the skyline with all four pooches and a backdrop of uninterrupted blue. The views back down the Lys valley on such a cloudless day were stupendous. The smaller mountains of Punta Telcio and St Anna frame Staffal, while the splendid summit of the Rothorn dominates the vista to the right of the valley. Lower down, the distinctive peak of Mont Néry, the tallest peak in the Frudiera range, is clearly visible.

From Cortalys, Footpath No. 7 carries on upwards through the larches. It passes the *Valle Salza* – one of the off-piste possibilities from the Punta Indren lift. Eventually, it meets the source of the Lys and the Monte Rosa glacier, which the Walser people thought of as the seat of Purgatory. They believed that the souls of the dead were visible on the mountain at night, with their pinkie fingers aglow like flaming torches; ringing bells to mark their steps. Occasional low, booming sounds interrupted the moody silence on our walk. We could see nothing, but suspect that it was the ice cracking, deep within the glaciers.

Instead of processing to Purgatory, we turned left and climbed past the houses to traverse the snow-covered pasture in front of the buildings. In summer, this area would be full of wild flowers and the sound of bells around the necks of the handsome chestnut and white Valdostane cows. A single milking goes to make the creamy D.O.P *(Denominazione di Origine Protetta)* Fontina cheese, a local speciality. (Valdostane cows also enjoy a good fight – but only with each other. *La Bataille de Reines – The Battle of the Queens* is a popular, springtime spectator sport, with crowds gathering to observe the cows' natural behaviour in establishing who's boss.)

Just past Cortalys, a small, wooden bridge spans

the river Lys. Rosie was not too keen; perhaps all this souls-of-the-dead stuff and the booming spooked her. She is also clever enough to know that trolls commonly lurk beneath such trestles.

We carried Rosie across, then clambered up a short, steep bank to join a woodland path. Designated Footpath No. 1, the route would become much more familiar later in the season as the exit to the off-piste itinerary *Bettolina Bassa*. In early January, it was quiet and as we walked past the only landmark, a deserted cow shed, we remarked that we were surrounded by all this beauty, but hadn't seen a soul.

The trail through the woods eventually joins Marmotte, a mountain road, which descends into the village. In winter, Marmotte provides a less steep but serpentine alternative to the red piste, Diretta Staffal. We call it The Zig Zag and it is another stalwart puppy promenade – a strenuous climb up through the trees, with fabulous views across the valley. Besides skiers coming down, its ascent is popular with snowmobiles, ski mountaineers and occasionally, fat-wheeled snow bicycles.

Since it was right on the doorstep of our residence, Footpath No. 7 became Mark's favourite option for The Pawsome Foursome's morning constitutional.

It was a shock, therefore, the following year, to find this preferred path blocked by an avalanche the height of a small block of flats. Tonnes of snow had been funnelled down the couloir where we had taken our Cavapoo photograph, while Mimma and Guido's boulder remained buried for the entire season. Suddenly, it was obvious. They would not have stood a chance. The debris contained blocks of ice the size of Fiat 500s and the boles of hundreds of fully-grown pine trees.

That autumn, on our way back from our travels, we returned to find Mimma and Guido's plaque visible once more. Nevertheless, we still had to clamber over what looked like a dam built by a giant beaver, using thirty-foot tree trunks. When we encountered the summer resident of our favourite, stone house in Cortalys, he warned us,

"In winter, the footpath on this side is very prone to avalanches."

We heeded his warning and thanked our lucky stars.

Our experience was a cautionary tale. An admonition that we needed to take just as much care about where we walked as we did regarding where we skied off-piste.

And while skiers carry A.B.S. airbags and give all kinds of advice about swimming upwards through a snow slide, it reinforced to us that the surest way to survive an avalanche is not to get caught in one.

The Walser people originated in the Valais in Switzerland, from which they took their name. Their traditional stone and wood houses, known as stadels, can be seen all over

Monte Rosa. In the Gressoney valley, Walser heritage means that German is widely spoken. Place names are shown bilingually in Italian and German, even though the official languages of the Aosta valley are Italian and French. On maps and road signs, Staffal is sometimes represented as Stafal or Tschaval.

4

A VIKING CHARM OFFENSIVE – & OTHER OXYMORONS

How to annoy people – including yourself

Bedtime saw us brimming with anticipation of an early start to get first tracks, but at midnight, our plans went horribly awry.

The Vikings arrived.

It gave us a sense of how the monks of Lindisfarne might have felt during the Norse raid of A.D. 793. We cowered in the dark as doors slammed, voices shouted and a thousand feet echoed as they stamped up and down the stone stairwell.

The dogs barked. To conceal our presence, we tried to silence them. Outside, the noise of scraping metal sounded like swords being drawn. *(The Viking mob was, in fact, rearranging a metal picnic table and chairs on the stone patio outside our bathroom window.)*

Once, Mark would have been straight out there; 6'6" tall and stark naked, shouting a demand for silence, like a Berserker at the front of a battle. But now, he is a new, mild and meditative mountain man, so he just lay there accepting that there is little to be done about a crowd of inconsiderate idiots. Especially when they're drunk and you're grossly outnumbered.

Aware of a brooding presence beside me, I assured him, "They will be quiet soon."

I was keen that he didn't take on what sounded like a ravening horde of heavily armed warmongers. They went quiet for a while, but then, as happens so often in battle, they got a second wind.

The sound of furniture being dragged across the tiled floors above us created the diametric opposite of a certain Scandinavian Furniture Company's 'Wonderful Everyday'. A symphony of Swedish voices accompanied the 'Atrocious Everynight'. Then, a reprise of the kerfuffle among the garden furniture. They went quiet again as a prelude for a half-hearted encore of slamming, scraping and singing before they were finally ready to settle down for the night.

I drifted into an uneasy sleep; full of night terrors. I wondered how long the Viking invaders might stay and considered the impact of sleep-deprivation on my skiing. Would they kidnap the dogs and use them as beards? Or would the sauna now overflow with naked Scandinavians, beating each other with twigs?

Like us, they didn't feel like getting up early. When they eventually arose, they sounded like the Roman Soldiers in *The Life of Brian*, running up and down the stone stairs in ski boots. That surprised us; we had laid odds that their manners and social skills pointed towards them being snowboarders.

As we opened our front door on to bright sunshine, we surveyed the devastation outside. The Vikings had left one of the garden chairs standing on top of a picnic table and had carelessly abandoned a single, empty bottle of *Leffe* beer on a windowsill. It was a good job that there were no traffic cones around, or it could have been carnage.

They were loitering outside as Mark took out the garbage.

"You should make a point by placing that *Leffe* bottle in the recycling bin. Right in front of them!" I told him.

He adopted the moral high ground (or maybe it was just because he was outnumbered) and nodded at them.

"Whassup?" he said.

"'Sup." They nodded back. There were six of them. Three of them were snowboarders.

I have pointed out before that the rivalry between groups is never so bitter as that between those with strikingly similar interests. Motorhome and caravan owners; windsurfers and kite surfers; snowboarders and skiers...

Snowboarders call skiers 'Pricks on Sticks'. I find this incredibly funny. It is far wittier than 'Wind W***ers', the phrase coined by kite surfers to describe windsurfers, although I appreciate the alliteration. Mark and I are far too polite and P.C. to retaliate with the phrase 'Gays on Trays', which rather usefully applies to both the snowboarding and kite surfing community. In any case, we are not prejudiced – we remain on speaking terms with a number of Wind W***ers who have transitioned to The Half Arc of Hades. There are baggy-trousered Shreditors with daft hats whom we are not ashamed to call 'friend', although we might draw the line at standing next to them in public.

I'm kidding. If you want an example of our liberal values, we once had a beer with a Shreditor *in a motorhome*.

Skiing, particularly off-piste, owes a lot of its recent development to snowboarding. Snowboards boast twin tips to ride in both directions and are shorter, wider and more shaped for sharper, quicker turns. As Twin Plankers, we salute the influence that Single Plankers have had on our sport.

Nevertheless, Mark and I do have some history with the skiing vs snowboarding conflict. Skiers and snowboarders usually regard each other with the sort of contempt that I would reserve for something really bad; like people who misuse apostrophes or put an s on *panini*. (For the record, *panini* is already plural. A horrible death awaits you for adding an s – and I will send the boys round if you even *think* of placing a grocer's apostrophe before it. I remain unaware of any comestible items who have committed to a life of materialism, so the requirement for a possessive apostrophe is rare-to-non-existent among perishable's. And before you say anything, I did that on purpose!)

Anyway, I digress. For us, it is not hatred, rather a wariness based on mutual suspicion and experience. I have had a few incidents during my skiing career and none have been with my fellow Pricks. Aside from hearing the scrape of doom behind you on a slope, there is no sense of dread that compares to getting on a chairlift to find yourself next to a snowboarder; or worse, sandwiched between two of them.

"Chairlifts are like Russian Roulette," a Powder Scraper admitted to me. This followed my being launched face-first into a snowboard-induced pile-up consisting of the human contents of three, four-man chairs because the liftie was too busy having a fag and being cool in his sunglasses.

Since I was looking the other way, I can't vouch for the circumstances that led to a snowboarder taking me out in Cervinia. It happened on a piste the width of the M6. I was motionless, waiting for Mark at the very edge of the piste. Thankfully, from the corner of my eye, I caught sight of something moving at the speed of an Italian overtaking on a blind bend in a tunnel. Had I not jumped instinctively into the air at the moment of impact, she would have broken both of my legs.

The fabric of my salopettes and knee brace are still etched with an eternal reminder of the coming together of opposing snow sports. As we extricated ourselves from our crumpled heap, she didn't apologise. Still, I am sure she was secretly pleased for me.

The razor-sharp, metal edge of her board had sliced straight through my padded ski pants and removed a chunk of my carbon fibre brace, thankfully leaving the fragile flesh of my left leg undamaged.

Mark took the pups out for their morning pee-poo run. Although he kept a watchful eye on everyone, Lani still disappeared. She ran the full length of the building, out of the garden and crossed to the other side of the piste.

"All I saw was a furry little black streak running back across the slope, dodging skiers," he said.

Little minx. Leaping in from the side of the piste without looking and getting in everyone's way, we were concerned that she might have self-identified as a snowboarder.

As a result of the nocturnal Viking invasion, we pushed back our deadline to lunchtime on the slopes. It was a sunny Sunday, so the resort was busier – there must have been at least half-a-dozen people on the pistes. We know from experience that the Italian weekend incursion from Milan and Turin skis in the morning, stops for around three hours for a slap-up lunch, then calls it a day. This is the time you want to have vacated the slopes, because they're all plastered.

The Vikings are less of a problem on the pistes. Wild eyed and independent, they are mainly found off-piste. They come to Monte Rosa as a warm up for the Scandinavian ski season, which starts around April.

Col d'Olen down to Alagna was deserted, although we quickly discovered why. My legs rebelled against this most challenging warm up; my first run of the day on a steep, very icy, 8km black run with a 1,768m vertical drop. Besides being quiet, the thinking behind our lunchtime ski was to make the most of the sun. Unfortunately, in January, the sun drops behind the mountains at around 2pm. In electing to visit Alagna in the afternoon, we had chosen to ski The Dark Side.

Mark was incredibly patient as I embarked on a mega faff. At the top of the Salati lift, there are no seats, so I went to the loo to remove the protective, rubber walking soles from my ski boots. As I came out, Mark was all ready to go. I still had the rubber soles on, as there were no seats in the loo – it was one of those rather disgusting stand-up facilities, sprayed liberally with who-knows-what.

"I'll help you take off the rubber things," Mark volunteered, knowing that I wouldn't want to touch them following their contact with a unisex toilet floor. "Then we can get off before that mob who've just got out of the cable car." I stood on one leg and then the other and we completed the operation with no-one falling over.

The view over the mountains was stunning. "Can I take a photo?" I asked. I got out the camera, then we had a fandangle getting in position for a selfie.

"Mark. I want you in it!"

"I'm behind you!"

"We're not in a pantomime..." although it began to seem like that.

"Which button do I press? Has it taken? Can you take it?" I demanded of Mark in quick succession. The answer, when it came, was decisive.

"NO!"

I put the camera away, but then discovered, "I've lost my gloves!"

I couldn't see them anywhere. They weren't on the floor, on my pole or in my backpack. I finally located them stuffed down the front of my jacket to keep them warm. Ready at last, I clicked on my skis and we set off. However, I had to stop almost immediately.

"I've forgotten to do up my boots!" Mark looked on but said nothing. I sensed that he wasn't angry. Just disappointed, which is much worse. We set off again.

"I'm cold. I've left my pit-zips open!" We stopped once more and Mark did up my underarm ventilation zippers. I couldn't see to do them with all my gear on and every time I tried to put my goggles up on to my helmet, they fell down the back. I apologised to Mark for being so annoying. I knew that I was being annoying because I was beginning to irritate myself.

"You *have* been *extremely* annoying," Mark said, "but I'm not annoyed."

I told you that he had morphed into a mellow, mountain man. What a guy!

Our skis scratched and scraped our way down to Alagna in the dark. I only dared to ask Mark if I could take one more photo. I know when I'm pushing my luck. We got the bubble back with Jean-Luca, a mountain rescue guide who works in Alagna.

"Your goggles have fallen down the back of your helmet," he said to me.

He told us that today was an annual public avalanche training day. "Can we go?!" we asked, excited. You can never do too much avalanche training, but Jean-Luca said that unfortunately, it would have finished because it started at 9am. The training covers different recovery techniques each time and this year was searching with dogs, which would have been fun.

My legs started to do what my mind asked of them as we skied down to what we call 'The Cuckoo Hut' at Bedemie. Filled with quirky wood carvings, the door makes a cuckoo sound as it opens and closes. It also serves the best *Bombardino* in the valley – a kind of warm, alcoholic eggnog. Just don't try to ski after drinking two of them. Although it was sunny, it was brutally cold, so we popped in for a coffee, a warm up and a slight communication problem.

Mark ordered, "*Due caffé, per favore. Molto caldo!*" - "*Very hot!*", because Italian coffee is often served lukewarm.

"Do you want tall ones?" the lady replied; straight back in English.

"*Si!*" Mark replied.

He was then served two coffees and two teas. Go figure!

The Seehorn chair carried us sedately back up the

mountain while we scoped out some of the off-piste routes beneath the lift that we had skied in previous years. Although they looked inviting, we shot back to the apartment as we were both pining for our doggies. On the lift, my goggles only fell off the back of my helmet another few thousand times.

Back at the apartment, we experienced the real *Game of Thrones*. Our thoughtful pups, delighted to be re-united with us, fully occupied the sofa, forcing their beloved humans to sit on the floor.

5

THAT MONDAY MORNING FEELING…

Matterhorn Materialisations, Abattoir Acoustics, & The Paw Perplexity.

Our full-scale Viking invasion continued to present issues.

The previous night, the Vikings had been a'viking once again. You might not know that *viking*, or more correctly, *vikingr*, is actually a verb. It is used to describe men behaving badly with beards and broadswords. Defined by this dreadful conduct, they eventually became known as 'Vikings'.

Like the Ancient Britons, we tried several techniques to tolerate the invading Viking horde. "They are from the land of the midnight sun," we told ourselves. "So, although it is dark, perhaps they don't realise that it is night and that others wish to sleep."

Acoustics is an oft-overlooked property of a stone staircase. Other than the Vikings with their strident singing and clamour of ski boots, I know only two other aficionados. These are *Led Zeppelin*; the *other* Fab Four – Messrs Paige, Plant, Jones and Bonham, and my friend's cat, Benjamin.

In the days before electronic wizardry, *Led Zeppelin* achieved the amazing, hollow sound on the drum track for *When the Levee Breaks* by recording it in the stairwell of an abattoir. *Stairway to Heaven* is on the same album. Perhaps by providing the real thing, the abattoir gave them the idea.

As for Benjamin, he is an operatic cat, although, like most artistes, he is very fussy about location when it comes to recitals. Benjamin lived for a time in a 400-year-old mansion and required the amplification and echo effects afforded by a historic, cantilevered stone stairway in order to perform.

We experienced a night of arpeggios. Whoops and yells reverberated around the masonry to produce a perfect *Nessun Dorma*. Not the famous Puccini aria; *Nessun Dorma* translates from Italian as 'No-one Sleeps.'

It was -17°C outside, but that is not why we closed the bathroom window. Our wish was to prevent any disturbance amid the garden furniture from interrupting our slumber. However, patio tables and chairs seemed to have been dropped from the Viking agenda. The cacophony of clattering from above suggested a large group playing *Giant Jenga* very badly, while simultaneously performing *Riverdance* in wooden clogs. Or maybe they just dropped a few Scandy-flat-pack wardrobes. Whatever the cause, even the cast of *Stomp* would struggle to better the Vikings for their volume and repertoire. The range of percussive effects coaxed from everyday items in a small, self-catering apartment was truly remarkable.

Although we had turned down the thermostat to 15°C, the lowest setting, closing the bathroom window meant that our room attained temperatures that would sustain Nuclear Fusion. The underfloor heating was particularly efficient. With every radiator switched off, drying our ski gloves presented a quandary. However, we discovered that placed upon a floor tile hot enough to fry eggs, they dried perfectly in no time. We just had to make sure that leather ski gloves and Mystery Muncher (who had already claimed the zip on my fleece *and* Mark's down jacket) did not come together.

Despite a poor night's sleep, we still arose at 6:30am with that Monday Morning Feeling. Sometimes, our pack greets the day with a howl to the tune of the alarm. Had there not been other guests in residence, we would have encouraged them.

Outside, the temperature plummeted to an uncharacteristic -27°C and our fingers stuck to the metal door handle. When they went out for their morning necessities, Rosie, Lani and Ruby whimpered and lifted their paws alternately, like frilled lizards, while Kai just lay down. This re-ignited The Paw Perplexity; "to boot or not to boot". Prior to our trip, we had agonised over doggie boots. Accepted wisdom suggested that dogs' paws are adapted to cope with different temperatures, so boots are unnecessary – and they don't stay on.

Nevertheless, we decided "to boot" and spent a few hours looking at doggie shoes, inaccurately measuring puppy feet and accurately re-measuring them. Then, we checked out *Amazon.de* in English and *Amazon.it* in Italian until we found the boots of our dreams, we hoped.

Some people despise *Amazon*, but global behemoths have their uses. *Amazon* has been a lifesaver during our travels. My *Amazon* U.K. account enables me to order from every worldwide marketplace, tells me what can be delivered to our location, and charges me in Pounds Sterling. This has facilitated the delivery of obscure and difficult-to-source items, such as laptop and camera batteries – as well as the sandals of my dreams – to campsites in the middle of nowhere. And now, sixteen doggie boots would wing their way up a mountain in a blizzard.

Once again, our deadline to ski had slipped back, although the Vikings were not entirely to blame. They had departed for the slopes at 8am, after treating us to a stairwell symphony of shouts. Deep snow posed a challenge for walkies. Since the nearby motorhome park was cleared of snow but devoid of campers, we took The Fab Four there for a game of ball.

It was a bright, sunny day, and following our stroll, we elected to ski over to Champoluc in the western valley. Conditions were perfect; it was like skating on soft icing-sugar until we reached Champoluc, where a sticky piste of man-made snow suddenly threw us off balance as it grabbed at our skis.

At Belvedere, which means 'Beautiful View', we stopped for a coffee at a mountain hut with the same name.

"Is that the Matterhorn?" I asked Mark, indicating a pointy mountain in the distance. "I think it is! Would you like a photo of it?" I gushed.

The reply came succinct and to the point. "No!" he said. "We have loads of photos of the Matterhorn!"

"But not from this angle!"

I skied on a little huffily, although, now that we had seen it, the Matterhorn seemed to follow us around. It started to appear everywhere; from the top of 'The Goat Run' (Sarezza); taking the lift back up to Gressoney – it was omnipresent. Unfortunately, being shadowed by a 4,000m mountain was not sufficient to take my mind off my freezing fingers. They were really beginning to hurt. The plan had been to ski over to the Cuckoo Hut at Bedemie for coffee and a slice of fruit flan, but I made a bold suggestion,

"Shall we just go home for coffee and see the puppies?"

Mark's answer came before you could even think, "Matterhorn". It was the exact opposite to his stock response whenever I say, "Can I take a picture?"

Our fur family tumbled out of the front door and played with us on the terrace in the snow. They got lots of fuss from Sylvia and a few guests, who wandered over from the adjoining bar. We refused several offers for each of them.

"I weel steel heem!" one lady said of Kai.

Sylvia confirmed, "They are becoming V.I.P. dogs!"

I couldn't deny it; we have always known that they are V.I.P.s – Very Important Puppies!

Once the pistes closed, we all went for a hike up the steep but nicely groomed black run, Moos, which was right next door to our residence. It was entertaining to see the pooches chase their ball up and down the hill. With so few walking options available because of deep snow, it was a good and tiring session for them. I opted for an energy-saving return to base by sliding down the slope on my behind. This was gigglemaking fun – until I realised that I couldn't stop.

It gave me the opportunity to practise my self-arrest; an essential winter mountaineering skill; "Kindly accompany yourself to the station, Madam."

Overnight, the Vikings subjected us to twelve hours of…silence. Joyous, quiet sleep with just the snow-muffled hush of the mountains. We even dared to open the bathroom window at 3am to reduce the temperature of our room to that of a glass furnace. The only sound was the tranquil chatter of the River Lys, subdued beneath her insulating blanket of snow and ice.

We had mentioned 'The Big Group' to Sylvia yesterday. Her immediate response was, "Noise?"

She said that she would have a word with their leader, Erik Bluenose or someone. Doubtful that it would help, we laid odds of 50:50 that Sylvia having a word would up the decibels. However, the Vikings clearly took on board that their popularity ratings were low. Perhaps they recalled that The Brits had defeated them utterly in 1066.

Remember Stamford Bridge, Erik?

Not the Chelsea stadium. The battle!

6

THE VIKINGS HAVE LEFT THE BUILDING

The Missing Minimercato, the Chimerical Castle & The Pervasiveness of Plastic Boxes!

Peace descended once more on the Lys Valley, once the Vikings had left the building.

Evidence pointed to a departure in the wee small hours following a decision to avoid anything mundane, like repose. Nightlife in our resort is limited – we did once see a person dance on a table in the bar, but that was an isolated incident and happened well before 8pm.

Sleep evaded me as the sound of Viking improvisation came through the walls. In the next room, someone turned a light switch on and off rapidly to produce disco-effect lighting. The stroboscopic result must have been a perfect accompaniment to the clattering, singing and what sounded like handfuls of marbles being scattered periodically across the tiled floor.

Noisy neighbours for a week are acceptable tribulations when skiing for a season, I suppose. With an arrow in the eye, Harold Godwinson's luck had been much worse in 1066. We trusted that William the Bastard landing an invading force of chaps called Norman, sporting funny haircuts, would not be the immediate follow-up to the Vikings' departure.

A sunny Saturday meant that it was busy on the slopes. With huge groups of half a dozen skiing around, we made an executive decision to go to Gressoney St Jean before the sun disappeared – and before the food shop closed.

Sylvia said that there was more choice in the shop two villages away in Gressoney St Jean, rather than Gressoney La Trinité, which was nearer. Going down the mountain also presented the opportunity for a warmer and less snowy walk for the dogs, so we dragged Big Blue out of the garage. As we descended the sunlit Valle del Lys, we admired the huge, frozen waterfalls that adorned her red-gold rock walls. The cathedrals of ice and fanciful scenery made me think of Narnia. To me, the Lys valley is one of the most beautiful places on earth.

Almost five-hundred metres lower than Staffal, Gressoney St Jean was noticeably warmer. A narrow path cut through the deep snow on the riverbank meant an easy walk for the dogs – and they didn't need their coats to keep the snow from balling up in their fur. As we walked along the river Lys, crystal clear water chattered over polished, grey rocks. Steep valley walls drew our line of sight straight up to the shining glaciers on the imposing, white monolith of Monte Rosa at the head of the valley. Above the snowline, we picked out tiny, summer hamlets, such as Alpenzu, high on the mountainside.

As we made our way into the deserted town centre, we could see very little; certainly, no supermarkets. The Tourist Information Office was swathed in darkness, but when we pushed our noses against the glass door, it gave way. Like classic Italian scholars, we entered with a flourish and asked, *"Dov'è il supermercato?"*

A grumpy lady replied, in Italian, that it is not a supermarket, but a mini-market and it was closed until 3.30pm. However, a few little shops, including a *Spar*, were open.

Two circuits of the village in Big Blue revealed no markets, mini- or otherwise. On the second pass, I spotted a fairy-tale castle, with five snow covered turrets, nestled in a forest on the hillside.

"Let's go there while we wait for the market to open!"

Our drive up the hill just added to the disappointment. *Castel Savoia*, summer residence of Queen Margherita of Savoy, was not even visible from the road. As if in a fairy-tale, it had disappeared into thin air.

Back in the village, we found two small stores,

neither of which looked like a *Spar*, but <*Drum Roll*> one was a shop that sold plastic boxes!

They say that you are never more than twelve feet from a rat. I can't tell you the relief to know that, even above 1,800m in the Alps, you're never more than twenty minutes from a shop that sells plastic boxes. Whether they cost £1 each, I can't say. Like every shop in Italy, it was closed. However, a pound, I found out later, is the going rate for a tin of butter beans in the mountains. Nevertheless, we were amazed and delighted to find a solution, should our improvised bed-base ever again be B.B.D.T. – Broken Beyond Duct Tape.

When we returned to the *minimercato* at 3.30pm, its doors were still resolutely closed. By now, we had lost the will to live and did a swoop in the supposed *Spar*. It had slightly more stock than the telephone-box-sized store in our home village, whose shelves are mainly empty. Even so, *Spar* could supply us with only a single bottle of milk.

Burns Night – 25th January – approached. To Mark's joy, it meant the annual rendition of my famous joke:

The Prime Minister visited a new hospital ward where every patient was spouting gruff and unintelligible sentences like, "Some hae meat!"; "Lord be thankit!"

The P.M. asked, "Is this a ward for people with mental illness?"

"No," the executive answered. "It's the Burns Unit."

I thank you.

We were packing a bottle of *Jura* single malt whisky. Although we had embraced it in earnest, we doubted that online ordering could furnish us with the traditional Burns night supper of haggis, neeps (swede) and tatties (potatoes) in the Alps.

In one way, our inability to buy food was a blessing. With our off-piste course looming ever closer, we both needed to get fit. And if I wanted to avoid a wet behind from skiing powder, I would need to be slim enough to fit into those pink pants…

You meet all sorts in saunas. Following our shopping trip, we went for a steam and ran into Svetlana and Artur, a Russian couple from Moscow, who were staying in Monte Rosa for a fortnight. We had a great chat, covering the baffling subjects of Trump, Brexit and how on earth we could spend three months skiing. It was a conversation that we decided to continue later over a beer.

Things went well over a beer. Then we got on to the *Jura*, at which point I started to expand my knowledge of Russian. As a bespectacled, pre-teen geek who liked to be different, I had once resolved to learn Russian. My strange desire was fuelled by a fascination with space travel, Uri Gagarin and a Russian folk song *Dark Eyes* – Очи чёрные, that I could play on the piano.

Artur and Lana couldn't understand my pronunciation, which was unsurprising. I was entirely self-taught from a Russian-English dictionary that I received for my twelfth birthday. A Scottish Gaelic speaker once told me that Gaelic (pronounced 'Gallic') is easy, "You just pronounce it exactly how it is written."

So, mountains in the Black Cuillin of Skye, *Ghreadaidh*, *Mhadaidh* and *Dearg* are pronounced just as they are written; *Hreetay*, *Vatay* and *Jerrack*, which is obvious, isn't it? Add in the Cyrillic Alphabet and you might appreciate my problem.

My Russian vocabulary of 'Yes', 'No', 'Beetle' and 'Uri Gagarin' increased by a large percentage. With Artur and Lana's patient help, I added *Nostrovia* – evidently a mispronunciation of *Na Zdorovie* – *На здоровьethe*, which means 'good health' or 'cheers'.

In a brain fogged by alcohol, I needed an aide-memoire and ran with the mis-pronunciation theme by co-opting "Nasty Rovers" to help me remember *Nostrovia*. The guys taught me the Russian for 'Arse', but by then, the *Jura* had disabled both short- and long-term memory along with my ability to speak.

The following morning, Rosie got me up at 7:40am on a false premise. I opened the door, then she and Lani played in the snow until my feet froze. Then we all went back to bed, which was not surprising, in the circumstances.

At 10am, we finally arose and congratulated ourselves on the sensible decision not to start the bottle of *Genepy* that Artur had brought. With amusement, we recalled Artur's statement that, "It's a myth that Russians drink a lot!" – although we had done our bit to uphold the British reputation for binge drinking.

Our new resolution of getting out to ski twice per day, made the previous day, had fallen at the first hurdle. My quest to get into my pink powder pants before our course, due to start in two weeks, had also been lost in a large quantity of beer, whisky and small snack items.

There was peace and quiet, but Svetlana and Artur told us that the Vikings' main party venue had been the room next door to them on the third floor. In the noise stakes, we, it seemed, had got off lightly.

We came to terms with the day as well as could be expected, following the demolition of a large quantity of whisky. Our puppy parcel arrived, so we made a first attempt at Pups in Boots. It was comical watching The Fab Four high-stepping and sliding around the apartment. Our walk in the snow to the head of the valley became an exercise in puppy boot retrieval. The boots disappeared almost as easily as the phenomenon that perplexed Lani when we threw snowballs into deep snow. "Where's it gone? Where's it gone?"

In the end, we gave up.

Boots may or may not be necessary, but experience supported the initial premise that we had read – they don't stay on.

7
WINTER WALKIES – LA PASSEGGIATA DELLA REGINA

We Walk in the Footsteps of a Queen

Founded in 1003, The House of Savoie (Savoy) is among the oldest royal houses in the world. And that fairy-tale castle spotted on our shopping trip to Gressoney St Jean was built for one of their number; Queen Margherita of Savoy.

Margherita was much-beloved queen. *La Passeggiata della Regina – The Queen's Walk,* was the route she used to take to the village from her summer residence, the Disney-like Castel Savoia.

Passionate about walking in the high mountains, Margherita was the first woman to climb Monte Rosa. She was also Honorary President of the Ladies' Alpine Club, affording some welcome credibility to women's mountaineering at the turn of the 20th century.

In August 1893, she reached Punta Gnifetti, one of the tallest peaks on the Monte Rosa Massif. At an altitude of 4,554m, the occasion was the opening of *Capanna Regina Margherita – Margherita Hut,* where she spent the night. The highest-altitude building in Europe, named in her honour, this mountain refuge has multiple elevated claims to fame: Europe's highest astronomical observatory; highest-altitude telephone connection; and with four hundred books in its library, the Continent's highest *biblioteca.*

Ever since it first opened, *Capanna Regina Margherita* has been a world-renowned research laboratory into high-altitude medicine. More recently, analysis of ice cores mined near the refuge have been used to study the modern issues of climate change, atmospheric composition and the spread of pollutants.

Our guide book suggested that we could link the *Passegiata* with our stalwart route along the river Lys to make a circular walk. It was time to investigate. Blue-blooded Princess Ruby certainly felt qualified to follow in the footsteps of a Queen.

From the car park at Gressoney St Jean, we crossed the pretty, wooden bridge to join the familiar Lys path. Initially bordered by trees, the vista soon opened out onto a high rock wall to the left, festooned with the jagged fangs of an enormous, frozen waterfall. Two kilometres further on is the hydroelectric plant (which is barely noticeable – so not quite the eyesore it sounds!) There, we would normally cross the river to return via the *ski de fond* and snow-shoe track across what is the golf course in summer. Instead, we continued over the main road to reach the village of Tschemenoal and clambered up past a farmyard filled with honking geese. There, we joined *La Passegiata;* Valle del Lys footpath No. 15.

The gorgeous, narrow trail winds through a tranquil pine forest, past huge boulders and secret caves. As we gained height, the views were stunning. The early afternoon sun caught the primrose-coloured villas and clock tower of Gressoney St Jean, making it shine like a city of gold in the valley below. From the Lys path, we had admired the Lyskamm glacier on Monte Rosa. As we continued in the opposite direction on the *Passegiata*, the snow-covered spires of Castel Savoia appeared, floating above a sea of lofty pines. All this beauty – and as usual in Valle del Lys, we had it all to ourselves.

We exited our own patch of woodland to cross an open area, which was evidently an avalanche chute. All the signs were there; only saplings dotted the slope. Every mature tree was bent or broken, or had its lower branches ripped off. Heavy snow had not characterised the season thus far, so avalanches were not uppermost in our minds. As we had been on Footpath No.7, we were shocked and chastened the following year when we found many of our regular walks, such as the Lys path and this part of the *Passegiata,* buried under avalanche debris over twenty feet deep.

The long, twisting driveway explained why Castel Savoia had not been visible from the road. As we climbed up first through pine forest, then through the Alpine botanical rock garden, five neo-Gothic towers greeted us. Fashioned from local, dove-grey stone, each turret is different, which adds to the surreal aura of the castle. Its architect, Emilio Stramucci, worked on other Savoyard buildings, such as the *Palazzo Reale – The Royal Palace* in Turin and a new stable block for the *Palazzo del Quirinale* in Rome.

Completed in 1904, Castel Savoia's royal period was relatively short. Industrialist Ettore Moretti bought the villa after Queen Margherita's death in 1926, then in 1981, it was purchased by the Valle d'Aosta Autonomous Region. Although the House of Savoy led the unification of Italy in 1861, it was deposed following the constitutional referendum of 1946, when Italy became a republic.

With a first female ascent, bountiful charitable works and Italian unification under Margherita's belt, it is ironic that the best-known legacy of this thousand-year-old dynasty is probably fast food. Legend has it that shortly after unification, Queen Margherita was on tour in Naples. Tired of fancy French dishes, she demanded pizza. Raffaele Esposito, the most renowned pizza chef in *Napoli* duly obliged and supplied a selection of *pizze*. Margherita's fave was reputedly very patriotic, sporting a simple topping of tomato, mozzarella and basil; red, white and green, conveniently the colours of *il tricolore*, the Kingdom of Italy's flag. And so, *Pizza Margherita* was born.

The House of Savoy still exists and is worth a

mention for its two Bad Boy royal cousins, who are locked in conflict for house supremacy and a non-existent throne. In the naughty corner is Amedeo, Duke of Aosta, while on the very naughty step is Vittorio Emanuele, Prince of Naples. Amadeo's reputed attribute of fathering illegitimate children is upstaged somewhat by the Hollywood blockbuster-worthy rumours surrounding Vittorio Emanuele: allegations of scandal, corruption and homicide, along with time in prison and under house arrest. And, apparently, Vittorio Emanuele punched Amadeo twice in the face at a dinner hosted by King Juan Carlos of Spain. Not quite the Royal fairy tale.

Once we reached the castle, we encountered a few problems of our own. Rosie suddenly seemed in some distress and occasionally cried in pain. The mere thought of a pea under twenty mattresses is sufficient for Princess Ruby to issue a screech that would shatter crystal. However, for stalwart, little Rosie, crying indicates something really wrong. We checked her over to see if she had hurt her leg or pulled a ligament, but a full-body prod gave no clues. Mark carried her all the way back down the hill into St Jean. Without muzzles, it was the one occasion where the bus driver would not allow The Fab Four to board, so Mark caught the bus alone and returned with Big Blue to collect us.

At home, Rosie seemed fine in herself, although now and then, she cried when we picked her up. She ate her dinner and some biscuits, so we were not too worried. But at times like these, every dog owner wishes their fur baby could talk and tell them what hurt.

Sometimes, the kindness of strangers really takes your breath away.

The following day, we discovered that the pain came from Rosie's tail. We found a small swelling and a slight kink near the tip, so we worried that it was broken.

"The vets in the valley specialise in livestock." Sylvia said, so she made us an appointment at the nearest small-animal clinic, an hour's drive down the mountain at Pont St Martin.

Matilde spoke no English, and my Italian is far from veterinary consultation standard. With a huge smile and extreme patience, Matilde listened to our pidgin description of Rosie's symptoms. She used her phone to translate English into Italian where my vocabulary failed, and Italian into English to answer our questions.

Rosie's tail was not broken, but she had a small haematoma between the vertebrae. Immobilised with a bandage, Matilde said that it should heal itself. It may not end up straight, but it was nothing to worry about.

Rosie wasn't in constant pain; her tail just seemed sore to touch. Matilde wrote an emergency prescription for anti-inflammatories, in case it got worse. Then she weighed everybody and provided a second prescription for their worm and flea treatment. She explained that she did not dispense; the human pharmacy in Gressoney St Jean would order the doggy medicine for us to collect.

Following the consultation, I could forgive Rosie for thinking that rather than the vet, she had just been somewhere to be fussed and loved, with a slight aside of tail-bandaging.

"How much do we owe you?" we asked.

"No charge!" Matilde said. We had taken up forty minutes of her time and were being dispatched with two prescriptions and a roll of bright turquoise *Vet Wrap* cohesive bandage. The rest of The Fab Four had also done rather well on the sausage front.

"Are you sure?"

We felt humbled when she had shown us such kindness, but she flatly refused to take anything for all her advice and attention.

Italy has gifted us so many fantastic experiences and memories such as this. The man who hopped into our car to guide us through the labyrinth of Verona's streets to our hotel, because the directions were too complicated. The Italian B&B owner who grated her son's night's work with his truffle hound over our breakfast, because, "You've never had eggs with truffles for breakfast? You MUST try eggs with truffles!"

It was just another example of why we love Italy so much – and why we are proud to call ourselves Born-Again Italians!

8
A DREAM DESCENT – THE HIDDEN VALLEY, DOLOMITES, ITALY

Skiing in a Whiteout, A Crystal Cliff & The World's Only Horse-Drawn Ski Lift

The Dolomites in north-eastern Italy has long been a spiritual home of ours; one that we have visited in both summer and winter. Although still part of the Alps, the curvaceous, blushing, Dolomite-limestone peaks have a very different character to the dark, granite teeth and pinnacles of the north-western Alps. Mark and I think of the Dolomites as female. UNESCO thinks of them as one of the most beautiful and unique mountain landscapes on the planet. Accordingly, they awarded the Dolomites World Heritage status.

In stark contrast to Monte Rosa, the 1,200km of pistes and 450 lifts in the Dolomite Superski area make it the largest lift-served ski area in the world. Despite the modern infrastructure, the culture and traditions are still well-preserved in the fifty or so charming villages, which are scattered through twelve valleys.

The Sella Ronda, a 26km circular tour around the Sella Massif, is the classic ski itinerary. Busy and crowded, especially on Fridays, when it is replete with ski schools determined to finish on a high, we tend to avoid it. Over the years, we have discovered alternatives. Unrivalled for their beauty, they usually lead to quieter and less well-known places.

A favourite of ours is The Hidden Valley, which often features in magazine compilations of 'the most scenic ski runs in the world'. It is definitely one for your ski bucket list, particularly if you experience it in the same conditions as we did on our first ever descent. Another unique feature to set it apart is the exit from the valley, which is via the world's only horse-drawn ski lift.

Access to The Hidden Valley is from the high point of Passo Falzarego, the mountain pass which connects the resorts of the Sella Ronda with swanky Cortina d'Ampezzo. From there, a cable car whisks you to the top of Monte Lagazuoi at 2,778m, where there is a choice of descents. The Hidden Valley is an 11km red piste. A black run takes you back to the lift station, or there is a quick way down via a sheer cliff face.

A hundred years ago, this area was the front line in a brutal war between Austria and Italy. *Vie Ferrate – Iron Ways* (singular – *Via Ferrata*) criss-cross the sheer sides of the mountains. Troops would use lanyards to connect themselves to these metal cables so that they could move safely in the precipitous environment. The *Vie Ferrate* are now used by recreational mountaineers to access places that would otherwise remain the realm of gnarly, multi-pitch rock climbers.

Inside the Lagazuoi mountain is a system of tunnels, dug out and inhabited by the combatants. During a previous summer vacation, we had clambered through these passages. At one point, Austria held the summit, while the Italians advanced from below. The Italian army captured the peak by tunnelling for six-months in order to plant thirty tonnes of explosives beneath Little Lagazuoi. They literally blew the top off the mountain, although the Austrians had either suspected their tactic or heard the works and had already withdrawn.

From our base in Arabba, we asked our rep for advice on how to get to The Hidden Valley.

"You take the bus from Armentarola," a purring tiger could not have rolled those r's as beautifully as Gabriella.

The visibility was poor as we skied over. The Sella Ronda circuit was closed, although since it was ski school Friday, we would have avoided the Sella pistes anyway. Few people were out, and we were left to cut our lonely trails through virgin powder, which had the texture of butter. I even elected to ski down a field of soft, fluffy moguls at the edge of one piste and was surprised to discover that I enjoyed it.

We located the bus stop at Armentarola with no hitches. On the bus, I found myself sitting next to an English guy, Dan, who introduced himself as a mountain guide with the company *Collett's*. He was escorting a family group down The Hidden Valley. With a sense of déjà vu, Dan and I realised that we had already met, during our summer climbing trip to the *Vie Ferrate* with *Collett's* two years previously.

The ride to Passo di Falzarego was a wild, uphill slalom into a howling blizzard, during which I tried to ignore the thousand-foot drops to the side of the road. Based in the mountains year-round, the violent weather made me appreciate the dreadful conditions that soldiers must have endured in the war. Even in the height of summer, the Lagazuoi tunnels had been cool and damp. To keep warm in winter, the men filled the trenches with straw, stuffed their boots with paper and rubbed their feet with tallow. Troops were issued with two pairs of woollen gloves, so that one could dry while the other was in use.

Due to the weather, we had been uncertain whether going so high was a good idea. From Rifugio Lagazuoi on our Via Ferrata trip, a 360-degree panorama had greeted us. It encompassed Cortina d'Ampezzo's principal ski mountain, Tofane, the glacier on Marmolada and the mountains of the Sella Massif, along with the dazzling pinnacles of Cinque Torre. When we alighted from the cable car in a gale of swirling snow, we could see nothing, other than Dan. All too aware of the quick way down from the top of Lagazuoi that we had observed in the summer, we asked Dan if we could tag along for safety. His group, Jonathan, wife Sally and son Hugo, agreed without hesitation. Like us, they were genuinely worried. Had they said no, the conditions dictated that we would have taken our Plan B – a return to Armentarola via the lift and the next bus.

The first part of the Hidden Valley is fairly wide, but steep. It was a joy to make gentle, sweeping turns through the untracked, knee-deep powder that covered the slope. We kept left on the red where the piste forked right to join the black run, which returned to the cable car. Once we dropped away from the summit, the immovable buttresses of Tofane and Lagazuoi sheltered us from the bitter wind.

The Hidden Valley narrows before twisting like a serpent through high rock walls. On a clear day, this affords views in many different directions, but today, everything was concealed and silent. Snow fell gently and quickly covered our tracks. Occasional soft, crystalline cascades slid from the branches of conifers that lined our way. Now and again, the mist parted to reveal the sheer, stone faces that enveloped us.

As we glided down past the only refreshment stop in the valley, Rifugio Scottoni, we turned a corner and there, the steepening piste took our breath away. A gigantic, frozen cascade covered the whole side of the mountain. It was a monumental temple of green, yellow and blue columns of ice, hundreds of feet high, which issued from holes in the rock. It was the most unique and otherworldly scene – and one that we enjoyed completely alone and in the enchantment of silence.

From there, we had to pick up some speed, as the slope flattened off before rising slightly. The final exit from the valley follows a frozen river bed. Here, you will usually be greeted by four or five horse-drawn sleighs, each with at least two lengths of knotted rope tied to the rear. If you are really lucky, your sleigh might be drawn by a team of Haflingers, 'The Golden Horse of the Alps'.

Haflingers are easily recognisable, since they share shades with U.S. President Donald Trump. Their bodies are spray-tan orange, with a characteristic thick, flaxen mane. Unlike Trump, though, Haflingers rock the look – and personally, I would rather trust a Haflinger with the future of the world.

For a couple of Euros per person, a sled will tow up to fifty skiers the last few kilometres to Armentarola. Throughout our descent, we had not seen another living soul. Unsurprisingly with the lack of custom due to the weather, the horse lift was not operating. This meant a very long and exhausting push with our poles to reach our route home.

Dan pointed out which pistes we needed to take for our return to Arabba but before we left, we treated everyone to a *gluhwein* – a hot, mulled wine, as a thank you. Had Dan, Jon, Sally and Hugo not allowed us to join them, our day would have been very different. Their kindness had given us something remarkable. Without them, we would never have experienced The Hidden Valley in such perfect snow and extraordinary peace.

We left our saviour and new friends at Armentarola to return to Arabba in deteriorating light. Meeting Dan had made a hairy ski so enjoyable that it still ranks among my top five favourite days on the snow.

Back at our hotel, there was a buzz in the bar. One chap, grinning from ear to ear, said,

"I've waited thirty years for conditions like today."

After hours of floating on powder, we went to dinner still feeling that gliding motion, as though we had been on a boat.

We have skied The Hidden Valley several times since, and have ridden the horse lift. It is a crazy experience, which never lacks a slight frisson of terror. The two parallel lines of skiers hanging on to their knotted ropes are hauled along a narrow, tree-lined path at a full-blooded canter. According to legend, carnage is not unknown, but on those occasions when we have yoked our destiny to the horse-tow, no-one fell. I guess like ladies' downhill legend Lindsay Vonn, sometimes, "Persistence is all that has kept me upright."

Every expedition to The Hidden Valley has been different and wonderful. The scenery is always breathtaking and the ice wall never fails to provoke child-like wonder. However, it has never felt so spellbinding and unique as it did on that lonely, misty, powder-filled, first descent.

The sensation that it gave us was something that we longed to repeat. This descent was what started our metamorphosis into Powder Hounds.

9
HOW TO IMPROVE YOUR SKIING IMMEASURABLY!

I used to cry on blue runs – here's how to go rapidly downhill from there!

"Would you like to ski down seven Chilean volcanoes for your fiftieth?"

Married to the skydiving, bungee jumping, White Water Rafting Queen, Mark already knew the answer.

The Magnificent Seven was how we discovered our tried-and-trusted way to get into the back-country safely. Before we booked ourselves on a flight to Chile, we realised that we needed to gain a few more skiing skills, as well as some mountaineering experience involving ropes and crampons. A head for heights would not go amiss – and I'm not sure that we could take the dogs... *The Magnificent Seven* might remain a dream, although our initial quest for these summits improved our skiing immeasurably.

A lack of proper tuition will hinder your progress

with any sport. *YouTube*, magazines, tips from your mates or instruction from a parent or partner have their place, although the last one is not always a route to domestic harmony. None of these produce the same results as a professional coach watching you and fine-tuning your technique. A good tutor also conveys the information in a way that is easy to understand and put into practice.

As windsurfing correspondent for the UK's *National Watersports Festival*, a question I am frequently asked is, "Which magic piece of kit should I buy to transform my windsurfing?"

My answer is that, while equipment plays its part, good, professional training will make the single biggest difference – followed up by practice. Plenty of practice. However, as we discovered, you must choose your tuition wisely.

On our initial visit to the freeride Mecca of Monte Rosa, we hired a local ski instructor to take us off-piste for the first time. We went up Bettaforca on our unsuitable, narrow carving skis. (Later, we were told that carving skis used off-piste are known as 'masochist skis'.) In deep powder to the side of the slope, our instructor wiggled down the mountain and shouted over her shoulder,

"You do it like this!"

That was the full extent of her instruction and safety briefing.

Our attempts to do it like that during the lesson failed. We tried to do it like that again in the same place the following day and Mark scored a grade three tear to the medial ligament in his right knee.

I think we can agree; that was €100 well spent!

The Volcano trip was how we first discovered the company *Snoworks*. Although we started a 'ski training' spreadsheet and have now gained freeride experience, I am not sure that South American volcanoes will ever feature on our ski itinerary. Nevertheless, *Snoworks* has facilitated plenty of wonderful adventures for us closer to home – and the all-terrain skills we learned have brought on our skiing, both on and off-piste.

Snoworks is a U.K. company run by Phil Smith and his wife, former Olympic downhill skier Emma Carrick-Anderson, along with their team of top-notch British instructors.

The daily rate for a week's tuition in Europe is not vastly different from hiring an instructor in resort. The crucial contrast for us was the certainty regarding the quality. Our first course also opened our eyes to the difference made by using suitable equipment. Appropriate off-piste skis are not only much more enjoyable to ride, they make the learning process a lot quicker, easier and safer.

The courses have left me with indelible memories of winter wonderlands as remote and inaccessible to most people as an expedition to the moon. I have seen deserted summer villages blanketed in snow around the back of Sainte Foy; skied fresh powder in the Dolonne couloir in Courmayeur; gone international on skis, crossing from France to Italy on the Petit St Bernard Pass, with wild boar stew for lunch as we sat on furs in a remote mountain hut. However, the ultimate descent has got to be the iconic *Vallée Blanche*; skiing the glacier beneath Mont Blanc.

I have advanced in age past my half-century and became a nervous skier following a silly fall at the end of a tiring day in Meribel. In bad light, I failed to see a bump on a nursery slope. I hit it at slow speed and fell over backwards. The back of my left ski caught on the bump and levered my left leg around, so that it ended up facing the opposite way to the rest of my body. The result was a trip to the legendary and appropriately-named Dr. Schamasch (pronounced 'Smash'). I returned from holiday minus one A.C.L. (Anterior Cruciate Ligament), but packing a bonus pair of crutches – and got three seats to myself on the flight home. After a long rehabilitation and a lot of saving up to afford a carbon fibre CTi2 leg brace to support my knee, I did eventually return to the slopes.

Mark was very diligent about protecting me on our next ski trip. He stayed so close that at one point, he actually crashed into me head-on and fell on top of me. He only weighs sixteen stone, though, so I hardly noticed.

Unfortunately, during that holiday, Mark and I were not the only ones who enjoyed a nice break in Italy. During the week, our group sustained a total of fifteen breaks – by which I mean a head count of fifteen. Some of the breaks were multiple; one chap broke his leg in four places.

Suffice to say that this did nothing for my skiing confidence. I left with the belief that sustaining a serious injury was an inevitable consequence of a ski holiday.

However, close friends of mine know that I don't like to be thwarted. I am a mountaineer with a fear of heights. A windsurfer with a healthy terror of being under the water. However, the thrill of these sports and the draw of the beautiful places they take me to has kept me in their thrall.

"I fell a thousand feet down a mountain – head first, feet first, every which way – and I just got up and skied off!"

Although Aunty Lilian reassured me that I had just been unlucky, it was tuition that fully restored my confidence. Mario set me on the path. The assurance of knowing that I can stop at will and turn when I want is a huge boost. Now, I am positive that I can cope safely with almost any conditions that the mountain throws at me. Steeps, ice, crud and deep powder are all within my capability – and I now concede that moguls deserve to exist. I might venture that sometimes, they are even to be sought out and enjoyed...

I also understand enough of the risks off-piste to be extremely cautious.

10

WITH GREAT POWDER COMES GREAT RESPONSIBILITY

How To Experience the Eighth Wonder of the World Without Killing Yourself

Before I take you off-piste with me, I want us to have a little chat.

Skiing in the unspoilt back-country, away from the crowds, in beautiful, soft powder is the eighth wonder of the world. Once you have tried it, I guarantee you will be addicted.

However, I do not want to underplay the risks involved. It is important to understand that with great powder comes great responsibility.

I cannot stress too strongly that skiing off-piste is dangerous and takes you into a very extreme and unforgiving environment. Sadly, every year there are fatalities. I do not recommend skiing off-piste without proper training, equipment (and a robust knowledge of how to use it) and a professional guide.

There is a whole science behind the study of snow and avalanches. Mountain guides train for many years to gain an understanding of the fickle mountain environment. I do not purport to be an expert; I am simply a skier who enjoys immersing herself in tranquillity and wilderness. My objective is only to highlight exactly what you are getting into the moment you stray from the groomed, patrolled, protected and marked piste.

It is essential to understand that skiing off-piste is inherently hazardous; you will never mitigate one hundred per cent of the risks. There are those who treat the mountains like a theme park and go out there regardless. But if you want to sample this unique sensation, how can you get out there without risking your life – or the lives of others?

A. Know the Risks:

1. The Mountain Environment

Avalanches, cliffs or crevasses, cornices, hidden rocks covered by snow – and other people – are among the main hazards. In ninety per cent of avalanche accidents, the slide is triggered by a person.

The death of three family members and their guide in Tignes – all properly equipped – was because skiers crossing above them set off an avalanche.

Regional avalanche risk data is published online,

although the offices of local mountain guides or ski schools often display details.

"It's ONLY Avalanche Risk 3!"

This epithet is oft' overheard in ski resorts – but Avalanche Risk 3 (on a scale of 5) still carries the description 'Considerable.' Are you happy to put yourself at 'Considerable' risk?

Many people are, which is why; "It's ONLY Avalanche Risk 3" is when most fatalities occur.

Be aware that avalanche forecasting is a science in itself. Prevailing conditions and slope aspect *(slope angles greater than 30° pose the greatest avalanche risk)* play a huge part in predicting localised hazards and are way beyond the scope of this short guide.

2. Self-Arrest – If You Fall, Can You Stop?

You need to choose your slope angles wisely, not only because of avalanche risk. If you fall, can you stop?

You will always stop once you reach the bottom of the mountain, cliff or crevasse – or if you hit a rock or tree. Whichever is the sooner. Even on piste, self-arrest is a worthwhile skill to have in your arsenal, just in case you do fall, although some slopes are strictly 'No Fall Zones'. Did you know:

1. On a slope angle of 35°: it is impossible to arrest a fall on hard snow.
2. On a slope angle of 45°: arresting a fall is unlikely, even in non-icy conditions.

3. On a slope angle of 50°: arresting a fall is impossible, whatever the snow conditions.

3. Minor Incidents Quickly Become Major Incidents

Aside from the obvious risks, remember that something as simple as a ski lost in deep powder, a broken binding, a dropped glove or even a minor injury can quickly turn into a major incident when added to a remote location and the cold. These are some of my own first-hand experiences of what can go wrong;

- *A guide skied down the 35° Eagle Couloir on one ski before poling for 2km to reach the piste. His client's ski binding broke shortly after starting the Punta Indren off-piste itinerary in Gressoney, so they swapped skis. What would you do in this situation?*
- *A friend broke her rib when an out-of-control skier dropped in recklessly from above and shoved her into the rock wall of a couloir. The helicopter could not get close because of overhead obstructions, so the rescuers had to abseil into the couloir and rappel the casualty out on a stretcher. The rescue took four hours. Apart from any potential complications from the broken rib, being immobile in severe cold for this length of time can be life-threatening.*
- *We spent forty-five minutes searching for a group member's ski, which released in deep*

*powder, miles from the piste. Although it took a
long time, thankfully, we found it.*

Although deemed 'definitely not cool', we wear powder tracers. You shove the loose end of these brightly coloured ribbons up your trouser leg and loop the other end around your ski binding. If your ski comes adrift in deep snow, you can find it immediately because of the ribbon lying on the surface. I admit that when you have to take off your skis for a gondola, tracers are a bit of a pain. Other than that, they are cheap, simple and effective – and in our view much cooler than getting stuck in the middle of nowhere with fewer than one ski per foot.

For a cool and much more expensive solution, various electronic ski trackers are available.

4. Weather & Route Finding

Mountain weather is very changeable and with no markers off-piste, it is very easy to get lost or disorientated, even in good weather. If you suddenly lose all visibility, you need to have a plan. If you don't know where you are, how can you call for help?

A man and his son spent all night on a mountain when they strayed off-piste into the wrong valley in perfect visibility. They had no phone signal and in the wilderness with no lifts, they could not get back before dark.

There are many websites to check weather before you go. It does no harm to look at more than one, since a forecast is just that; a prediction. It is not an absolute. There can also be very marked local variations, so don't forget to take a peek out of the window!

As windsurfers, we are used to constantly checking and comparing forecasts and a little of our windsurfing wisdom also applies to skiing;

"If in doubt, don't go out!"

The mountains will always be there tomorrow – and if you are careful, you will be too.

B. What to Carry;

In the event of an avalanche, ski poles are best discarded, since they can drag you down, so we don't use the wrist loops off-piste. Our poles also have large powder baskets fitted to the end, to stop them sinking in deep snow. We never venture off-piste without a transceiver (which we check every time we turn it on), shovel and probe (which we know how to use – and with which we practise regularly.)

For a ninety per cent chance of survival, you need to locate and then dig someone out of avalanche debris, which sets like concrete, within fifteen minutes. Any longer and the likelihood increases rapidly that the casualty will suffocate and you will recover a corpse. In the event of an avalanche, you will not have time to work out how to use your equipment or conduct an efficient search, particularly if there are multiple burials requiring rescue.

Our backpacks also contain snacks, water, extra clothing, spare gloves, goggles and a lightweight, emergency shelter. Just in case. If you are crossing glaciers, you need sufficient knowledge and the correct climbing equipment to perform a crevasse rescue.

Plan your route and leave details of where you have gone and when you expect to be back. Carry a detailed, topographical map (not a piste map!), a compass and program the emergency number and your insurance details into your mobile phone. Do this even if you're with a guide. When venturing into extreme environments, you must take responsibility for yourself – and that means acknowledging that your guide is neither immortal, immune to avalanche burial, nor bulletproof when it comes to injury.

C. Are You Insured?

The *Ski Club of Great Britain* insures us, so we are certain that we have cover for ski-specific risks. Most ski insurance policies *do not* cover you for skiing off-piste *at all*. Some offer cover only if you are with a qualified guide.

If you venture off-piste without insurance, sweating about how you might raise the tens of thousands of pounds required to pay for your helicopter rescue and medical bills should keep you warm in the snow. Even if it takes a few hours for help to arrive.

In these cynical days, you might even be asked for your credit card or proof of insurance upfront, to demonstrate that you can pay, before being given succour or medical attention.

D. Skills & Skis

Skiing off-piste requires different skills and skis as well as the essential safety equipment mentioned previously. Skis for carving tight turns on piste may be as narrow as 60mm underfoot and will sink in powder. You will not always be able to use your edges to carve turns in deep snow off-piste, so you will also need a few extra tools in your skills box to tackle the varying conditions that you will find in the back country.

My *Kastle LX All Mountain Skis* are 92mm underfoot – they cut through slush and are a joy to ride in a variety of conditions. My *VÖLKL 100Eight Powder Skis* are – you guessed; 108mm underfoot and float like a hover-board in deep snow. Mark and I have also undertaken many courses to ensure that we possess the skills needed to read and cope with variable terrain.

I have been mountaineering since I was a child. Nevertheless, the training has reinforced my already healthy respect for the mountain environment.

E. Conclusion

Get out there and enjoy the unspoilt back-country – there really is no sensation to compare. However much of a thrill it offers, though, it is not worth risking your life – or the lives of those forced to come to your aid. So please treat the mountains with the respect that they deserve and always err on the side of caution.

11

ADVENTURES OFF-PISTE DAY 1 – GRESSONEY BACK-COUNTRY SKI COURSE WITH SNOWORKS

Tinkering with Transceivers & Descents with Dave

"You will need skis at least 100mm underfoot" said *Snoworks'* chief instructor Nick Quinn at our welcome meeting.

Mark and I felt like the luckiest off-piste skiers in the world. A week previously, thin lines of white piste were framed by grass, while the black run, Moos, needed a bit of a strim. Then it started snowing. And snowing and snowing and snowing. The visibility over the weekend had been terrible, but Monday morning, the first day of our off-piste ski course, brought blue-bird skies, no wind and thirty centimetres of fresh snow. Hence, Nick's recommendation for fat, floaty skis.

Our Back-Country Course alternated full days of instructor-led, all-mountain skills training with off-piste adventure in the company of a mountain guide.

Day One started with lovely, lovely Dave, a Scottish guide, based in Chamonix, with whom we had skied a number of times.

While it is very satisfying to have the skills to cope with whatever the mountain throws at you, the holy grail sought by most off-piste skiers is powder snow.

Gliding through soft powder in the muffled silence and solitude of a total whiteout is my most treasured memory from our first ever *Snoworks* all-mountain ski course in Tignes. I could have been alone. Everyone else was hidden in the murk and the only sound was the gentle hiss of snow against my skis, like fine sandpaper being drawn along a skirting board. I felt like I was floating; the sensation made me giggle to myself.

Suddenly, through the pale, white silence, spontaneous whoops of joy and laughter erupted all around me. In that moment, I grasped the draw of powder. The Hawai'ians considered riding waves on the ocean a religious experience; powder surfing down a mountain is exactly the same.

It was a collective epiphany. Through crisp, virgin snow, fellow student Paul barrelled up to where Mark and I had stopped. Slightly out of control, he collapsed in a flail of skis and poles at our feet.

"I know I fell over," he said, "but that was the best thing I have ever done in my life!"

Straight away, Dave found us beautiful, soft powder

underneath the Seehorn lift. After picking our way through, we crossed the piste and dropped into the trees opposite on a route that we had skied with Dave a few years previously. The snow there was so soft and deep that it flew over our heads. It would have been easy to kid ourselves that we had somehow been transported to the Land of the Rising Sun and were skiing the fabled Ja-POW.

Despite the recent new snow, the base cover was not deep and I fell quite a few times. I put it down to first day nerves; skiing defensively with my weight in the back seat. I focussed on keeping low and maintaining my vision one metre downhill and two metres behind. This is a spiffing trick that stops the skis from running away from under you (which happens more as your weight drops back and un-weights your tips). It gives much better control, especially on steep slopes.

From Passo Salati, at the top of the Gabiet gondola, we did a wonderful descent, passing beneath the lift pylons to enter the remote valley beneath Orestes Hütte, a mountain refuge which is accessible only off-piste. According to *Fall Line* magazine, Orestes rates Number One among the 'Five Most Luxurious Mountain Huts in the Alps'. On our way down, we met the warden, who told us that the hut was open, but Indren was closed. (The Indren lift serves only off-piste itineraries.) He mentioned a walking trail to Orestes Hütte – which I filed away mentally under, 'something fun to do with the dogs'!

The warden advised that after new snow, the

pisteurs like to allow twenty-four hours for the layers to settle and bond. Today, below 2,300m, the avalanche risk was Level 3 ('Considerable') and Level 4 ('High') above. We proceeded with caution.

As we descended the Endre valley and passed the entrance to the narrow couloir *Leisch*, Dave pointed out some large, slab avalanches released by skiers who had traversed high. One was on a convex slope. He indicated that it had separated because of surface hoar. Exactly like the hoar frost that you see on winter mornings, surface hoar is moisture from the air which freezes on to a surface. The hoar had produced beautiful, lacy patterns on top of the snow. However, the danger with surface hoar is that it doesn't bond with new snow, so it causes a very unstable layer, which rarely improves with keeping.

Dave explained why we were safe standing next to the convex slope,

"The tension released when the slab broke away, so it won't slide now. Snow on convex slopes is notoriously unstable, because it's already under tension due to the curve. Even without an unstable layer, it can break away easily when subjected to any stress, such as a skier passing over. It would have been safer for the skier to have avoided the convex slope altogether and taken a route underneath, through the bottom of the gulley."

We returned to Passo Salati and skied down Col d'Olen on the Alagna side. At Pianalunga, the mid station, Dave asked if we wanted to stop for a coffee. The unanimous response from our group was,

"Waste this powder. NO WAY!"

Following some recent confusion that I had developed regarding the North/South divide, I asked Dave's advice on assessing avalanche risks connected with slope aspect.

"It's not that easy," he said. "You need to look at it. There is no hard and fast rule about south facing slopes being unsafe; sometimes the sun's heat followed by freezing overnight stabilises them, although it doesn't necessarily make them nice to ski on. Anything well skied should be fine, since you are only dealing with new snow, but you must treat convex slopes and large open faces that haven't been skied with caution."

We put his judicious advice straight into action. Rather than dropping in at the top of Olen, we entered the col just under the historic Rifugio Guglielmina, to assess the traverses and slopes before we were committed.

More untracked powder on the left side of Salati returned us to the café under the Gabiet gondola station. By this time, we were all shattered. We had planned to meet another group for a 1.15 lunch, but it was 1.45 by the time we arrived.

A long, tiring morning meant a short afternoon. Our final off-piste descent under Indren took us to the perfect location for our avalanche transceiver training. If you ski off-piste, the safety equipment that you should carry as a minimum is an avalanche transceiver, probe and a shovel. Not only that, you should know how to use them blindfold, in your sleep or with one hand tied behind your back.

Avalanche safety kit is not rocket science, but it takes skill and practice to use. The transceiver is simply a radio beacon with a 'transmit' and 'search' (receive) setting. It is worn beneath clothing, so that it can't be ripped off in the maelstrom if you're caught in an avalanche. To locate a skier buried in an avalanche, rescuers switch to 'search' and use the distance and direction readings from their transceivers to locate the signal from the casualty.

The probe is a telescopic pole, which allows the searcher to prod deep into the snow to locate the exact position of the victim. 2 metres is a suggested minimum length, but if you consider the potential snow depth in an avalanche, the longer the better; ours are 2.4 metres.

The shovel is to dig out the victim. Physical shock during an avalanche knocks the crystalline arms off snowflakes, allowing them to settle more densely. In addition, friction melts their surface slightly, so that when they come to rest, they freeze together instantly. This is why avalanche debris sets like concrete – and why a sturdy, metal shovel with square shoulders that you can stamp on is recommended.

I mentioned earlier that suffocation becomes a real possibility within just fifteen minutes of being buried in an avalanche. If you lose a comrade (or comrades), there is no time to wonder how to work your transceiver or conduct a search. While you hope that you will never have to use your search and rescue skills, you can never hone them too much. To react in an emergency, when you are also likely be suffering from shock, a transceiver search must be second nature.

Our drill was to use a transceiver and probe to locate a buried backpack containing a transceiver. I was the first to go and managed to find the burial in four-and-a-half minutes. I would have preferred to be quicker, but I took fewer than fifteen minutes, so the backpack lived!

This ordered and organised search contrasted markedly with a rather shambolic avalanche training exercise in which Mark and I took part with a ski club in Flaine.

Skiing is not a cheap sport; something that is reflected to an extent in the character of those who take part. The avalanche search operation illustrated this beautifully. It was a microcosm of group dynamics, and demonstrated perfectly the inability of the management classes to listen, take direction and work together.

Our avalanche search protocol is;

1. Take charge.
2. Try to visually mark the last known position of the casualty.
3. Call the emergency number to summon help.
4. Switch transceivers to 'search'.

5. Do not swing your transceiver, hold it close to your body.
6. Search in an orderly, grid pattern.
7. When the transceiver indicates that you are near the victim, place the transceiver close to the snow. The closest reading may still show that you are a few metres from the victim due to the depth of the burial.
8. Use your probe to see if you can physically locate the victim.
9. Dig on the downhill side – the priority is to clear the face.
10. Change diggers regularly, since digging is tiring. Give them something else to do.
11. Keep other people with transceivers away and manage the situation.

Simple enough, but this was how it played out with too many chiefs.

We were divided into three groups to search for three buried 'casualties'.

"Right. Switch your transceivers into search mode," instructed our self-appointed leader.

We all obliged, although one person managed to fail in this most elementary of tasks.

"Who still has their transceiver on transmit?" All three search parties were now locked on to the signal from one of our number, rather than the buried casualties. It took a while to discover the numpty.

"Oh. You wanted me to switch it to *search*!"

We had already lost a few of our precious fifteen minutes.

Our instructor had placed three ski poles in the snow as the 'last known sighting' of our victims. Rather than conducting an ordered search downhill from this point, the three groups fragmented into cliques and sauntered off chatting and doing their own thing. Some searched with transceivers; others randomly stabbed the snow with their probes. Some had been unable to work out how to extend their probes. A few took off their skis and sank in the snow, then struggled to put their skis back on.

The three search groups intermingled, so one casualty had no searchers, while the others were pursued by a stampede worthy of Ladies' Day at Ascot with free prosecco. Our self-appointed leader was ignored. Anyone who tried to instil any form of order was treated with disdain. Older, grey men ignored other men – and would certainly not take instructions from a woman. The female attitude to any attempt to assume leadership was, "Who do they think they are?!"

The milling search teams looked for all the world like competitors in *Monty Python's* 'Upper Class Twit of the Year' competition.

It was entertaining to witness; these were traits that Mark and I had encountered so often in our working lives. Folk who are, 'Far too busy. Far too important'. They cease listening to instructions about twenty per cent in, because they already know EXACTLY what to do. The sobering part was that on this trip, in an accident off-piste, these were the people on whom our lives would depend.

This is the stark reality that could so easily play out in an emergency. On this occasion, all the backpacks perished.

Cause of death was; "I know best!"

On the homeward leg, Mark and I peeled off at the black run, Moos, while the rest of our group went for an après ski drink. We couldn't wait to see our doggies – and they were inseparable from us once we got back. Sylvia had looked after them for us and said that, although they had been very good, "They cried a little."

That broke our hearts. Mark and I had been away for a full day. It was the longest that we had ever been apart from our pups.

Nevertheless, there was a sense of triumph in the air. Wonderful views, beautiful snow and best of all – I had managed to squeeze my behind into my pink pants. In combination with my pale green jacket, I had been returned to my off-piste Powder Chick persona of the Pistachio and Pink Peril.

Everything was at one with the world.

Rifugio Guglielmina

At 2,880m, Rifugio Guglielmina, 'Europe's Highest Hotel' was world-famous and renowned for having 'The Best Wine Cellar Above 2,000m'. Part of the folklore of Monte Rosa, we discovered it on our first ever stay in Gressoney. Stuck on the Gabiet gondola for forty minutes when it broke down, we got chatting to Tone and Peter, a lovely, Danish couple. Guglielmina was off-piste and we weren't sure exactly where it was, so they guided us there for lunch. Although they were in their seventies, we couldn't keep up with them on the icy traverse!

Tone and Peter knew the Guglielmina well and ordered the house specialities on our behalf. On a sunny terrace, sheltered by tall, three-storey ochre walls and surrounded by mountains, we enjoyed cheese and ham pancakes, dried meats, then gnocchi for the girls and stinco – slow-cooked, aromatic pork shanks – for the boys. We finished with blueberry pancakes. The accompanying drinks were a sensation. Peter explained the secret code,

"You have to ask for the wine from under Francisco's bed!"

The twelve-year-old wine was soft and tawny, made from the same grape grown at three different altitudes. Mark and I had carefully researched Italian wine vintages on a recent road trip through Barolo and Chianti, so we knew that it came from an exceptional year. The pear liqueur that complemented our dessert contained 20kg of pears per litre. It was intense and beautiful.

Throughout lunch, Peter cradled Tone's hand. It was heart-warming to see; after a lifetime together, they were so obviously in love. So kindly, they insisted on treating us to lunch, then told us,

"You can stay the night in the refuge and see the sunrise – then you will understand why they call it Monte Rosa."

It went straight on the bucket list.

Later that year, on 22nd December 2011, I called Rifugio Guglielmina to book our stay, but there was no answer. A quick check on the internet to make sure that they were open over Christmas revealed the breaking news that the refuge was on fire. Thankfully, everyone escaped to safety, although high winds fanned the flames and hampered fire-fighting efforts. We forgave them for not answering the phone.

The magnificent refuge was almost destroyed. It had been in the Guglielmina family since they built it in the late 1800s, but, because of its high, mountain location, rebuilding is too costly. It is so sad that something so unique and wonderful has been lost, but I am grateful that we experienced it. I shall always treasure the memory of that random meeting and the perfect, sunny afternoon that we spent there in warm and wonderful company.

12

ADVENTURES OFF-PISTE DAY 2 – DON'T MISS THE TURN OR YOU'LL GO OVER A CLIFF

Eagle Couloir, Bettolina Bassa & Canale Grande

The dogs knew.

A 9.30am rendezvous with our instructors in the next village, Gressoney la Trinité, put our morning routine on a tight timeline. In order to arrive on time, we had to feed and walk The Pawsome Foursome, have breakfast and get ourselves ready with all our paraphernalia to catch the bus at 8:50am. Because the pups sensed what was afoot, all four decided that they needed to be hand fed. Lani would only take her food one tiny piece of kibble at a time.

It was Tuesday and today, we were Team Richard – a second day with a mountain guide. The Indren lift was open, so after a quick warm up on piste, we ducked under the hallowed portal at the top of Passo Salati. We passed the warning sign that says 'danger of death' and clanged our way up the metal steps and poled our way to the cable car.

It always feels slightly reckless and exciting to duck under barriers and leave behind the world of mortals; of crowds, groomed snow and marked slopes, to taste the forbidden fruit of off-piste joy. The cable car rose to 3,275m, high on the glacier and when we stepped out, past a device that checked our transceivers were working, we had the mountain to ourselves.

The day did not disappoint. We had *Canale dell'Aquila – Eagle Couloir* for breakfast, *Canale Grande* for afternoon tea, with *Bettolina Bassa* sandwiched in between.

The horrible wind-slab at the top of the Indren lift took us all by surprise. It looked like powder, but had a thin crust that broke and grabbed at our skis. The stop-start pull of the snow threw us right off balance and rather uncharacteristically, I was the only one not to fall. I panicked when I looked back up the hill to see Mark flat out, with one ski poking up out of the snow like a thin tombstone, miles away from him. He didn't get up.

"Mark is the sort of guy who will say he's OK with one arm hanging off." I told Richard. "He skied for half a day with a torn ligament because he didn't want to make a fuss…"

Thoughts of the terrible injury sustained by Michael Schumacher made me glad that Mark wasn't wearing the headcam today. Mystery surrounds the circumstances of the severe brain injury sustained by

Schumacher in a skiing accident in the French Alps. Some speculate that it was related to his head camera – either the mounting inflicted the damage or weakened the helmet, causing it to shatter on impact.

When Mark got up an age later and skied over to me, he told me he could see stars. He had landed heavily on his head and neck, but mercifully in snow, not on a rock.

"That's the *worst* snow I've ever skied!" Mark said later.

"You've led a sheltered life!" Richard replied. "At least you can turn in it!"

That was a matter of opinion.

Today, my skiing improved, but as I got tired, I started falling again. Yesterday, I had been leaning backwards and uphill, into the mountain, which was why I kept sitting down.

Eagle Couloir is a marked off-piste itinerary, so it is usually well skied. It is narrow, with a maximum gradient of around thirty-five degrees and faces southwest. These factors usually conspire to it being filled with ice and moguls, although following the blizzard at the weekend, then Indren's closure the previous day, we were rewarded with the most fabulous, soft snow.

Our second route was *Bettolina Bassa*, a steep sidevalley, accessed from the top of the Bettaforca lift. The descent, so far from the slopes, immersed us in the forlorn beauty of the remote mountain environment.

The *Bettolina Bassa* route cuts away from the pistes through a wide basin of pristine snow, with majestic views across to the blue-white glaciers of Monte Rosa. It then drops through a steep couloir with rocky walls and cuts to the right on a narrow path through a forest. Although not steep, the path posed the greatest challenge. It was icy and had the added hazard of thinly-covered rocks and elder bushes to rip off your skis. Even our guide, Richard, fell victim to their grasping fronds. Since it was so narrow, speed control was difficult and as we joined the red Marmotte piste, two large humps propelled us into orbit. We recognised the humps – they marked the last stand of Mark's rotator cuff. He fell there two years ago with his arm outstretched. It took a shoulder operation to put things right.

Throughout the day, Richard regaled us with good advice. As we tackled *Canale Grande*, he said,

"Don't fall. If you do, you won't stop sliding until you hit the bottom – or a rock. Whichever comes first!"

From *Canale Grande,* we opted for the sporting exit. We abandoned the easy traverse back to the Gabiet lift to drop down a near vertical powder slope. Then, we cut through *Leisch*; a steep-sided canyon, known anecdotally as 'Middle Earth.' Here our guide offered further sanguine advice,

"Control your speed and don't miss the turn at the end, or you'll go over a cliff."

Some of the elementary skills that you thought you left behind in your first week of ski school are invaluable weapons in your off-piste armoury. Side slipping and stem turns, where you pick up one ski to change the edge, are great ways of negotiating terrain where there is limited room to turn. We used them all in *Leisch*.

Leisch is tricky; a narrow, rocky, icy chute followed by an iPod (Icy Path of Death) through trees. Mark loves trees. He ended up astride one.

The final part of the exit, back on the piste through the Moos valley, was almost flat. I hatched a plan; get up a bit of speed so I wouldn't need to pole. Female downhill legend Lindsay Vonn's advice on extreme speed is, "If you back off things go wrong."

As usual, I overcooked it, but lost my bottle and backed off half way down. I crashed in a puff of powder. Falling in powder is usually fun; like landing on a feather duvet, although if you sink, it's difficult and exhausting to get back up. The trick is to cross both of your poles in one hand and push against the increased surface area.

My poor skis were not so fortunate. They had clanked all the way from the top of Indren because the metal protector on the front of one had come loose. By the time I got back to the valley, the protector was lost forever.

Thankfully, this was the only casualty of elder bushes, ice and multitudinous wipeouts.

However, the experience made me feel a little poetic. If you are sitting comfortably, I shall begin;

Ode to Lost Ligaments & Other Injuries.

I lost my A.C.L
In Meribel.
Mark's Medial took a corker
When he fell on Bettaforca.
And skiing a bit too fassa on an icy passa
His Rotator Cuff got a batter on Bettolina Bassa.
I thank you.

13

ADVENTURES OFF-PISTE DAY 3 – STEEP & DEEP

Euan, 'Eureka' & Eagles.

The tactic of placing a few slivers of grated cheese in the pups' food helped to divert them from the hand feeding issue. Our fur babies saw us off with a look of resignation rather than reproach, but we still struggled to leave. After two full days skiing off-piste, The Big Mommas and their bouncing babes had been back. It was Wooden Wednesday, a midweek sensation familiar to all skiers – our legs felt so stiff that we found it difficult to walk.

Our commute to work on the Jolanda lift was through a whiteout. The top was obliterated by a blizzard. My first sight of the morning was Nick, *Snoworks'* Chief Instructor, skidding plumes of powder snow over his head on the black Jolanda 1 piste. Whooping with excitement, he shouted,

"Look at *this*!"

Today was our first day with an instructor, Euan, rather than a guide. I had an immediate 'Eureka' moment. I mentioned to Euan that sometimes, my downhill ski juddered.

"You jam your downhill leg out straight. It's a defence mechanism, but it's counter-productive because it pushes you off balance and makes you lean into the hill."

That also explained why I kept sitting down.

At the top of Indren, we asked for advice on tackling the windblown slab that had caused such problems yesterday.

"Ski like you're on eggshells, but if you break through the crust, be firm." Euan advised. "You want to ski either on top, or through it."

My second descent of Eagle Couloir felt much more controlled, although Mark struggled a bit. Yesterday's heavy fall had dented his confidence.

Eagle's thirty-five-degree slope provided an excellent place to practise skiing steeps.

"The key is to get your downhill hand below your waist to weight the downhill ski – and keep your visual focus just below."

We know from windsurfing (and every other sport in the world) that vision is critically important. You need to look where you're going. When skiing, that is downhill.

If you have ever skied into a tree, ridden your mountain bike into a boulder or collided with any obstacle, anywhere, you will understand the importance of 'vision' in sport. There is only ever one reason why you crashed into it. You were looking at it!

And I'll wager that, just before impact, your last thought was, "Oh my God... *Oh my God!* I don't want to hit *that*..." Then you hit it.

It's called target fixation.

My advice is simple. Next time you find yourself travelling at high speed towards an immovable object, *don't look at it*. Look elsewhere. Do that and I *guarantee* – you will miss it.

Anyway, back to steeps. I was first down and stood with Euan to watch the rest of our group and a few other skiers coming down Eagle. His analysis of every skier who passed was the same;

"Hand above the waist."

"Hand above the waist."

"Hand above the waist."

"Hand above the waist..."

It seems I am not alone in my bad habits.

We took the lift from Gabiet to Passo Salati, intending to ski Col d'Olen into the next valley. The dreadful visibility precluded any consideration of venturing off-piste, so we skied blind down the marked black run. Even that proved difficult. Unable to see a thing, a safe descent required us to deploy every tool in the box. Euan suggested not making too many turns and gliding to lose height and conserve energy.

I strained almost as much to see the piste markers as I did to remember whether the longer orange tops indicated markers on the left or the right of the slope.

(The usual protocol is that the pole on skiier's **R**ight has the o**R**ange top!) Mark's goggles seemed to have steamed up between the lenses, so he was having real problems. They had been a free gift with a magazine subscription, so we didn't feel too frivolous about replacing them. Once we got to Alagna, it was a relief to buy a pair of functioning low-light goggles in the ski shop by the lift station.

Exhausted, Mark and I decided to go home at lunchtime. It took us well over an hour to get back in the whiteout, even though we know every twist and turn of the Salati piste. As a little girl, I remember my Aunty Lilian telling me about being caught in a whiteout while mountaineering,

"I didn't know if I was going uphill or down!"

"How stupid!" I thought. How could you not know that? Surely, you would feel the strain on your legs if you were going up. Now, having experienced a whiteout, I can tell you that it is one of the most disorientating experiences that it is possible to have. With no horizon or other visual references, it is definitely impossible to know whether you're going uphill or downhill. It is also impossible to determine whether you're stationary or moving, or even if you are standing upright. More than once, I have fallen over in a whiteout simply because I couldn't tell whether or not my body was perpendicular to the surroundings!

Euan's plan for the afternoon was to take the rest of the group to ski in the trees at Seehorn, since trees provide some helpful contrast in low light conditions.

By the time everyone had eaten lunch and skied back over, we reckoned that at most, we would have missed only a couple of runs.

Eagle Couloir had been fun, although today, even there, a lot of the powder was on top of slab. Euan concurred that some of the snow that we skied was, "horrible!"

At home, we collapsed beneath a blanket of warm puppies and nursed our broken bodies. I virtually had a bath in *Zheng gu Shui* (literally 'bone setting water') my failsafe Chinese rub-on medicine. A godsend discovered in my martial art days, *Zheng gu Shui* is a warming balm, which removes bruises in a flash and cures all known aches and pains.

Despite our commitment to safety, we couldn't summon the energy to drive down to Gressoney la Trinité for the evening session, which was an avalanche safety briefing. Instead, we re-energised ourselves in front of the T.V. with a bottle of wine.

14

ADVENTURES OFF-PISTE – A BETTER BETTOLINA BASSA

Powder Skirts, Hoary Hair & Face Plants

Our bus ride to the meeting point at Gressoney la Trinité had been through dense fog. However, as we rose from St Anna to the top of the Bettaforca lift, we emerged into a landscape that sparkled in the sun.

Soft powder glistened under a cobalt sky, while tiny flakes of blown snow added a touch of magic. They hung in the air and twinkled, like a golden sprinkle of fairy dust.

Today we were Team Nick – *Snoworks*' chief instructor. On our very first *Snoworks* course, Nick had told us, "You learn more if you smile. It's a scientific fact!" All I can say is that he must have learned a lot in his life, since his countenance is never anything other than a broad beam. His enthusiasm and smile are always infectious – and his grin was wider than ever when he saw the conditions.

The plan was a re-run of *Bettolina Bassa*. We descended the combe and the steep couloir with much more finesse, although Mark's right ski upstaged us all. It took the record for the longest solo descent.

Rather than the high traverse beneath the rocky cliffs, we followed a different line to exit the route. The final pitch involved a thirty-nine-degree slope, covered in bushes. Grasping branches pulled off Mark's ski. Once it gained its liberty, it raced even nippy Nick straight to the bottom. Like Bode Miller at the Men's Combined Downhill in Bormio, it forced Mark into a heroic, one-legged descent. I was in awe.

The lower path through the trees was a little less daunting than the track we had taken with Richard a few days before. More snow cover meant that, although it was similarly narrow and winding, it was not so icy – and the rocks and bushes were less prominent. It was enchanting; sliding through the silent, snow-blanketed forest with the sun winking between the trunks. Nick laughed with joy as he knocked the branches with his ski poles as he passed. Like showers of sparks, snow cascaded around us in the sunlight. It was magical.

Our descent of *Bettolina* was a wonderful moment, captured just in time. A malevolent cloud had followed us down from the summit. Half an hour later, we would not have chosen to ski the route, which made it all the more special.

For lunch, we headed over to *Campo Base – Base Camp*, a Himalayan lodge at the top of the Mandria lift.

Heralded by an array of colourful prayer flags outside to bless the mountain, we call it 'The Tibetan Hut'. *Campo Base* serves wonderful, home-made pasta. You can even sample Tibetan lunch specialities on Tuesdays, although I haven't tried them. In Nepal, my experience of cuisine from 'The Roof of the World' failed to wow me.

While my compatriots wolfed down a full-English to prepare for our day's exertions in the Himalaya, I decided to be adventurous. I don't learn. My Tibetan breakfast challenged me with a smörgåsbord of delicacies, each of which incorporated rancid yak's butter in some form. Even my cup of tea was not spared; it came to me salted and covered by a greasy slick of tainted dairy product from the hairy bovid. (You might be surprised to know that this is still not the worst cup of tea that I have ever had. That honour goes to Ecuador, for the lukewarm, milky, dishcloth-grey concoction, full of lumps and membrane, that I was served near Otovalo.)

On our way there, off-piste in impenetrable fog to the left of Bettaforca, I did my *best ever* face plant. In the low light, I hit a hidden dip. I flew straight out of the front of my skis and landed face-first in a perfect starfish sprawl.

Although my jacket has a powder skirt, I'd had snow up my jumper most days. Today, there was snow down my neck and, in my goggles as well. Sadly, Nick missed my airborne antics and no-one caught it on camera. However, a panel of witnesses beheld the grace and beauty of my launch and flight, concluded by the finesse of my nose-first touch-down. Unanimously, they awarded me a perfect ten.

On the way home, we tried some jump turn drills. Jump turns are a useful tool in the all-terrain arsenal. A jump allows you to turn within a ski's length in tight spaces. On steeps, it helps to avoid picking up excess speed, while in deep or heavy snow, it releases the edges of your skis to enable you to turn.

We had learnt so much. I felt so fortunate that, instead of going straight home and back to work after the course, Mark and I could perfect all these skills and drills in the weeks to come.

As we dropped back to the village in the murk, Mark pointed out that my plaits had turned to ice. In Puccini's *La Bohème*, Rodolfo sings "Your tiny hand is frozen."

My tiny hands were fine – but I did have hoary hair!

15
ADVENTURES OFF-PISTE – THE INDREN INVERSION

Don't even think you will get an edge in that...

The gods were conspiring against me. When I drew the curtain, I saw... nothing. Thick mist concealed the landscape, right to the base of the mountain. Mark decided not to ski. He was exhausted and had pain in his back and neck following his heavy fall on Tuesday.

I am sure that the emotion of leaving the pups for another full day also played a part. It was understandable; I felt exactly the same.

Kai is a sweet and sensitive boy – we often say that he is not a dog, he is human. Kai didn't make things easier. Although he had his Dad with him, whom he adores, he still sat in front of the door, big, brown eyes pleading with me not to leave him again. Rosie made her feelings known by snuggling up on my ski jacket as if to say, "You're forgetting something... MEEEEEEE!"

I trudged my lonely path to the bus stop to find the

road blocked by a broken-down piste machine. Six men were trying to roll up its caterpillar tracks and load the beast on to a lorry. It didn't matter, since the bus to take me to my rendezvous at Gressoney la Trinité failed to turn up. I was so disappointed. Once I had decided to go for it, I was reluctant to miss the final day of the course.

I plodded despondently back to the apartment. Following a game of telephone tag, I got a message to Kathy, our mountain guide for the day, and we arranged to meet at The Cuckoo Hut for coffee at 11am. The numbers in our group had dwindled – there was just Tom and Judy today. They told me I had only missed a gloomy morning in the trees and, with a bit of poetic licence, skiing on a cliff.

After a few runs in pea soup visibility, we took the lift to Salati to check whether Indren was clear. It looked rude not to, so we attacked *Canale Grande*, since we had already skied the adjacent Eagle Couloir twice. Kathy worked so hard to find us fresh tracks and at the very top, pointed out ragged, wind-blown snow formations called *sastrugi*. They were noticeable even in the poor light. Their deep, sapphire-blue hue shone out as though they were lit by L.E.Ds. It was the only hint of colour in the entire dead, monochrome panorama of grey that surrounded us.

The visibility did not improve on the way down, but I was skiing out of my skin. Everything seemed to have clicked. The late start and coffee appeared to have given me fresh legs and enabled me to link my powder turns and concentrate hard on getting that downhill hand low.

At the bottom of *Canale Grande*, we stopped for lunch at Orestes Hütte and were introduced to The Boss. Huge and handsome, he is a silvery-grey Norwegian Forest Cat, who presides over the establishment. At least the same size as our Rosie, the largest of The Fab Four, he regarded us with his amber eyes and posed regally for photographs.

Orestes is a magical place. Far from the main ski area, it is a cosy, wooden chalet tucked beneath the sharp peak of Piramide Vincent. Powered by hydroelectricity from the stream and with drinking water from a spring, Orestes serves wholesome, vegetarian and vegan food. Its location was chosen by two skiers. Since Indren has featured in *Fall Line's* 'One Lift for the Rest of Your Life', its position in such a paradise of back-country ski routes is no surprise.

I treated myself to a warm, chocolate pear tart. Not bad at 2,600m, in a refuge so remote that Judy laughed when I asked how you might get your luggage there if you stayed overnight. Kathy was very diplomatic,

"If you don't ski in, you could probably come up by snowmobile. But they have everything here that you would need."

After lunch, I made an observation,

"The sun's coming out and that's not just Lancashire optimism talking!"

We clicked on our skis and pushed ourselves along

with our poles. With the weather improving, we decided to take another crack at Indren.

"It will be nice to finish on a long run!" said Kathy.

The schuss out through the valley from Orestes is fairly flat and I scared myself a bit. I picked up more speed than I intended on the steep downhill section that leads down from the Hütte, but unlike my barrelling adventure other day, I remained upright.

"I would rather pole than go too fast!" Judy was far more sensible.

Really, I should learn. As a teenager, I remember scoring two black eyes and Frankenstein-style cuts to the face by riding my bike at high speed into a brick wall, via a rose bush. All in an attempt to save energy.

My friend lived on a hill. I came to grief by concocting a plan to cycle up to the house without pedalling. The aim was to gain sufficient momentum on the downhill approach to coast all the way back up. However, I mismatched the curvature of the drive with my, by now, extreme velocity. As a result, I didn't quite make the bend...

"That rose bush is in *just* the wrong place!" My friend's brother, Alex, consoled me. Alex spoke with the voice of experience. Obviously, I was not the only idiot who had tried to free-wheel uphill and misjudged the corner.

The top of the Indren lift was cloaked in brilliant sunshine. The mist that hid the valley below from our sight was caused by an inversion. Usually, air temperature decreases with altitude but an inversion happens when a layer of warm air traps cooler air beneath.

Kathy made an executive decision to go off to the right on a route called *Diretta Indren*. New territory for all of us, it was a fabulous descent with beautiful powder pitches interspersed with rocks, if you got off the path – and a waterfall.

"Don't even *think* you will get an edge in that!" said Kathy, indicating the glassy curve of water ice that bent over the drop. "You'll be straight down…"

The view from the top of the waterfall summed up everything that I love about being in the back country. A mountain wilderness with no-one in it but the four of us. We looked down like gods from the heaven above our world. Lit by the sun, a crown of snowy peaks projected through the cloud inversion. It was just us and nature; tranquillity and solitude; a peaceful majesty so rare, isolated and exquisite.

We side-slipped tentatively down the edge of the waterfall and took in our options.

"Do you want to do the long traverse or go down here?" I looked at the rather precipitous slope that greeted us and made a suggestion on behalf of the group's tired legs.

"Shall we do the long traverse?"

One at a time, we crossed a wide, avalanche-prone slope, with the prescribed thirty-metre space between each person. When traversing an open face, leaving a large gap is a precaution that ensures the fewest casualties if an avalanche does occur. Usually, but not always, the first skier triggers the slide. Separation ensures that other members of the group will be spared to raise the alarm and carry out the search and rescue for those unfortunate enough to be buried. Once we had all traversed safely, we stopped beneath a rocky cliff, a break in the terrain which would provide a safe refuge from a snowslide. From there, the way down looked rather inviting.

"I think we'll get some fresh tracks here!" Kathy said.

Kathy went first, then filmed us bouncing down the beautiful powder slope in unison. It was the most incredible finish to a fabulous week.

We dropped into the inversion to reach the exit and more than once, we shared how glad we were to have a guide. Heaven only knows how we got out.

"It's useful that they put poles out to mark the itinerary," I said to Kathy.

"That's the piste!" Kathy replied.

Only then did I notice a huge snow-making machine looming in and out of the gloom. The visibility was so bad that we had somehow lost the traverse line and ended up poling through knee deep powder, albeit always in the right direction. Kathy and I stood at the edge of the piste making comedy foghorn sounds to attract Judy and Tom, who were invisible in the gloom.

That evening, we were treated to a film show of our trials and tribulations, filmed by Nick. It was sad saying goodbye to our fellow skiers and all the guides.

However, there is no sensation like the feeling of triumph as you ski home after yet another fabulous day in the wilderness, knowing that you have challenged yourself, achieved more than you believed was possible and made memories that will last you a lifetime.

The Italian icing on the cake was that Sylvia had looked after the pups all week. She had taken them on different walks every day, "to make it interesting for them." When we offered her something for her trouble, she emphatically declined any payment because,

"I was here anyway!"

16

EXPERIMENTS ON THE EDGE OF CONTROL

The Gauntlet Goes Down on the 80mph Club

"The fastest I've done is 128km per hour. That's almost 80mph!"

"Really? That's about the same as me!" claimed a youthful American accent, concurring with London. Both a little too loudly for the confines of a crowded gondola.

"You need the right kind of slope. One that is steep and then flattens off," London added, for everyone's benefit.

Such claims should not go unchallenged, but our eyes met and we kept our counsel. We didn't really want to bother to engage or discuss the fact that with speeds like that, they should be in the Olympic team.

As we alighted from the gondola at Passo Salati, Mark whispered in my ear, "There was a strong smell in there."

"What do you mean?" I asked.

"Of bullsh**..."

Some things need not be spoken between man and wife. With not so much as a glance between us, we watched them ski off as we faffed around, tightening the buckles on our boots and clipping on our skis. It is always nice to observe what technique Bravado chooses when out skiing on hired equipment. Without a word, we both knew exactly how this would play out.

We overtook them easily. Mark, it seemed, had forgotten how to turn. He simply pointed his skis downhill and went like a rocket, parallel, straight down the black run. Well. It was the right kind of slope. It was steep and then flattened off.

I slipped past them on the inside of the first bend. We kept the pressure on, since we didn't want them to catch us up. 8km later there was no sign of them as we quietly clipped off our skis at the bottom of the piste in Alagna. As we rose sedately in the gondola to Pianalunga, we saw them walking along the road towards the lift.

"There's the 80mph club!" I said to Mark.

No doubt they were discussing the fact that there is no slight to your masculinity in being left for dead by two fifty-somethings after bragging about how fast you are. Even when one of the fifty-somethings is a girl.

Part of the thrill of our favourite sports, windsurfing and skiing, is teetering on the edge of control. That feeling that you are nailing it – just – but knowing that one false move and everything will go horribly wrong in an instant. When you are pushing the envelope; that's when the adrenaline really kicks in.

Our Valkyrie ride down the black run, Olen, to Alagna had blurred that edge today. It had shifted our thrill radar from control firmly towards speed. We were bristling with the need for excitement, following our taste of forbidden fruit during our off-piste course. So, we decided to ski the resort from end to end and back – and managed it in three and a half hours. Not bad when we were held up by a long queue that meant we missed not one but two full cable cars at Pianalunga.

We skied the black, Moos, as though it was the *Hahnenkamm*. I went so fast that I actually took off over the brow on one of the pitches.

"In control?" Mark asked.

"Um. Not exactly!"

Of course, pushing the limits to this extent was only ever going to end one way. On a chairlift, we were complimented on our 'His 'n' Hers' *Kastle* skis. That was very topical, since it just followed our 'His 'n' Hers' fall. Flying down from the top of Salati, I went for The Full Monty. I caught a ski edge and dropped my pole as I cartwheeled through the air, before sliding down the mountain head first and on my back. This vantage afforded me a great view of Mark, who was following behind me.

He decided to do the gentlemanly thing and pick up my pole. Since he was almost on top of it and moving like a bullet, it was always a plan of spectacularly daring ambition. As I looked across the slope and caught his eye, he was suspended in free-fall on the other side of the piste. We slid in unison, laughing like lunatics. It was our first fall on piste for two-and-a-half months and who knows? Careering down the mountain on our backsides, we might even have hit 80mph.

Well. It was the right kind of slope!

17

A DREAM DESCENT – THE VALLÉE BLANCHE, MONT BLANC, ITALY / FRANCE

Fresh Tracks from the Highest Peak in Western Europe

Tucked beneath Mont Blanc and nestled between Chamonix and Courmayeur, The *Vallée Blanche* is the most famous and iconic off-piste route in the Alps. It is also one of the most beautiful. 20km long, with a vertical drop of 2,700m, it is a mountain wilderness, isolated behind the impenetrable bastions of legendary Alpine peaks. Although it is an off-piste itinerary, it is not the most difficult. Most guides will say that it is within your capability to ski if you are competent on a red run, although don't let this delude you into thinking that it is safe. The route passes over a glacier, whose crevasses shift constantly; your skiing ability is irrelevant if you fall into one.

For many years, it had been up there on our ski bucket list, but there was a snag.

The classic access to the *Vallée Blanche* from the

Aiguille du Midi cable car is via the *Arête du Midi*. A precipitous spine of snow- and ice-covered rock, from which people do fall and die.

Mark and I both have a serious phobia of heights. Skydiving, bungee jumping and rock climbing are just some of the ways we have tried to overcome it, but still, the prospect of carrying our skis across a knife-edge ridge in slippery ski boots filled us with horror. While we were desperate to ski the *Vallée*, fear plagued us; could we cope with the approach? And what if we froze? For months, we tormented ourselves.

In the weeks leading up to our Courmayeur back-country course with *Snoworks,* I sent out a plea to my mountaineering friends on *Facebook*.

"The *Vallée Blanche* via the *Aiguille du Midi Arête*. Who has done it? How bad is the walk in (if you suffer from vertigo?!) I need a sanguine appraisal."

We knew that it was possible to avoid the treacherous *Aiguille* and enter the *Vallée Blanche* from the Italian side. However, research suggested that while we were there, the lift to Punta Helbronner at 3,466m was closed for renovation.

Snoworks' Director, Phil Smith, reassured us about the *Aiguille*. It would be a shame to miss out on such a once-in-a-lifetime experience, he said,

"The sides are not vertical and the distance is relatively short. A couple of hundred metres. Normally the guide ropes everyone together. Once across this you can ski and the run is moderately easy but spectacular. The guide can place you directly behind him/her and there is absolutely nothing that can go wrong. So that's it. Nothing to worry about and a great descent."

In resort, we received the best news ever.

"We're going in Spaghetti Side!" Giddy with excitement, I broke it to Mark. "Helbronner is open!"

Wednesday was the day, but as it approached, our relief began to look academic. The forecast predicted heavy snow and whiteout conditions, which would make skiing the *Vallée* impossible. Yet, the biggest surprise still awaited.

On Wednesday morning, I pulled back the curtains of our hotel room in Courmayeur to be greeted by birdsong. Mont Blanc was resplendent in sunshine, beneath a perfect, cornflower-blue sky – and half a metre of fresh powder. The weather front had passed through overnight. I hardly dared to hope; today, we might ski the *Vallée Blanche*.

At our rendezvous at *Hotel Cristallo* at 8.30am, we received the stunning news; we were on.

The instructors divided us into groups; we were Team Pete, which put us with The Bristol Two – Andy and Peter, along with Welshman, Paul. Since we were skiing on a glacier, we were all issued with climbing harnesses. These would facilitate rescue, should we fall into a crevasse. Not that we would, of course.

The sense of anticipation was palpable on the bus to the Helbronner lift. As we ascended the steep faces of Mont Blanc on two successive cable cars, our guide, Pete, talked us through the views and shared his story.

"I studied poetry at university. Then I came to Chamonix and decided that I needed to spend the rest of my life climbing!"

Through the panoramic windows of the cable car, we saw a skier launch off one almost vertical face and set off an avalanche. It was like watching the live action from a *Warren Miller* extreme film. At the top of the lift, a strange contraption shot our skis to the top in a bucket, while we climbed a steep metal staircase. In the thin air at 12,000ft, our ascent of three-hundred steps soon became a breathless slog.

From the viewing platform on top of the world, we gazed out over a roll-call of the most iconic Alpine peaks and climbing routes. Pete pointed them out with reverence; the Matterhorn, Monte Rosa and the flanks of Mont Blanc – the three highest summits in Western Europe. He indicated the spiky, granite pinnacles of *Les Dames Anglaises*,

"I bivouacked there during a two-day traverse of the ridge."

It made me dizzy to even think about it.

With our skis secured to our backpacks, we walked beneath the giant red and white cranes that were building the new Mont Blanc Skyway lift – a feat of engineering almost as jaw-dropping as the views. On *Col Flambeau*, we followed a snow track and clicked on our skis opposite what I call the unofficial *Dent du Geant – The Giant's Tooth,* a granite finger that prodded the azure sky. There were lofty peaks all around and most excitingly, like royal icing on a wedding cake, pristine, untracked powder sloping off in every direction.

"It is truly a privilege to be in this environment." Pete said.

My thoughts were captured on video, "This is already the best day of my life!"

Pete's safety briefing brought us back to earth.

"We'll get fresh tracks, but just stay within the swath that I'm setting. Keep an eye out for holes. There will be times when you want to be right in my tracks."

Amid this beauty, it was easy to forget that we were crossing a glacier – an extreme environment. The main danger was falling into a crevasse, which might be hidden under snow.

"Don't ski anywhere but where I tell you. Always stop above me; there might be a hazard beyond. And if you fall into a crevasse, don't struggle. You will likely get hung up by your pack," Pete reassured us. "And don't take your skis off. Ever."

"Have you ever performed a crevasse rescue?" we asked.

"Only one. A snowboarder stopped for lunch a little way below the group, then tried to walk back."

Pete's final piece of advice was, "Relax, square your

shoulders and let the first turn come to you." And with that, he was off.

In the soft powder, we needed to push hard with both skis to turn. We giggled like children as we floated down *Combe de la Vierge – The Virgin Combe,* leaving joy in the air and fresh, wavy trails in the pure, untracked snow.

As we moved towards the towering spire of the *Aiguille du Midi* on the opposite side of the valley, the French itinerary *Jontion* joined from Chamonix. Here, the terrain changed to a steep, icy mogul field. Pete turned effortlessly on the tops of the bumps, then led us on a long traverse beneath the *Envers du Plan* glacier to *La Seraccata – The Seracs*. These immense cliffs, columns and shards of blue, glacial ice looked like shimmering, faceted crystals. Hundreds of feet high, they had been formed by an icefall; a break in the glacier as it rippled over a drop and splintered into a craze of deep crevasses.

Above us, the Refuge de Requin mountain hut provided a most incongruous stopping place for those plagued by a sudden desire for hot chocolate in the midst of an icy desert.

Just beyond *La Seraccata* is *La Salle a Manger – The Dining Room*. Here, safe from the hazards of avalanches or toppling seracs, but with skis firmly on, we stopped on an icy hummock for a picnic lunch. Paul grinned as he announced that, "Now, there's a part of a foreign glacier which will be forever Wales!"

The scale of the landscape was humbling. The

snowy wilderness sparkled in the sunshine with the backdrop of crags and towering summits. Two or three other *Snoworks* groups were in the valley, along with who knows how many others, yet we could not see another soul. The only sound in the stillness of the mountains came from a flock of inky-black Alpine choughs, who chattered around us, looking for an easy meal. Mountaineering folklore suggests that choughs are the winged souls of climbers departed.

Like a grimy tide mark on a student's bathtub, the glacier's lateral moraines had left their impression high above us on the valley walls. The sad thing was that they show the level of the glacier in 1860; not so many years ago.

After lunch, we continued to the *Mer de Glace – The Sea of Ice*. The descent had now flattened. We suggested to Pete that we could just sit where we were and let the glacier carry us down to Chamonix.

"Some guided groups do move in Geological time!" Pete affirmed.

Side valleys, hanging valleys and smaller glaciers dotted our route, while crevasses reminded us where we were. At one point, we saw a perfect pointy peak surrounded by a rim of cloud, exactly how a cartoonist might represent a mountain in *The Beano*.

Pete urged us to drink in the last of the views as thick cloud began to roll up the valley. It was amazing to be encircled by soaring peaks on such a beautiful day. It reminded me of so many other of my favourite mountain days, where the immensity of nature just left me in awe. As we dropped into the fog, Peter caught an edge, which exacerbated a calf injury that had been bugging him for a few days.

"My calf is hurting a bit," was his only complaint, despite us finding out later that the calf injury was a ruptured Achilles tendon!

We caught up with another group, who told us that the snow was poor lower down, with bare rocks protruding. This, along with Peter's plight, helped make our decision to take the train back to Chamonix.

As we skied on into the impenetrable, looming mist, we were glad of our guide. There were still several awkward traverses to negotiate and rocks to avoid. On one, I praised the dire visibility – and the sharp edge-grip of my skis. It looked like a 'no fall zone' to me; a solid block of ice with a boundless abyss disappearing off to the left.

Shortly after, we took off our skis and strapped them to our backpacks. We clambered above the abyss into an ice cave. Frozen shards on the floor clattered like broken glass as we stepped over them. My ski boots had little purchase on the steep slope; I stuck to the rock climbers' first law of 'maintain three points of contact' each time you move.

Inside, the ice cave was amazing. The glassy walls must be hundreds of years old and glowed deep blue, even in the dull light. Unfortunately, a photo of all the shadowy figures carrying their skis as they made their way up steps hacked out by ice axes was out of the question. Today of all days, both our stills camera and head camera batteries had run out before we even started our descent.

To climb into the cave, we had to straddle a hump of snow and ice. As he leaned forward, Paul's skis, jutting upwards from his backpack, dislodged a handful of icicles which dropped down his neck. I got stuck astride the tumescence. Because of the brace that I wear due to my ligament injury, I can't flex my left knee fully. A French chap dislodged me. He shoved my leg over the bump in unison with Pete hauling me bodily. It was anything but elegant!

Then came the steps. Pete said,

"There are five hundred of them. Well less than that. Four hundred and ninety-seven or something..."

The scary thing is that each year the glacier recedes, so more steps must be added. Originally, the *Montenvers* train was at the same height as the glacier. As we toiled and clanged up the metal stairs in our ski boots, tourists coming down from the train to view the ice cave regarded us as though we were extra-terrestrials. Along the way, placards announced the level of the glacier, according to the year. This climb should be compulsory for every climate change doubter. The loss of glacial ice between the years 1990 and 2000, merely a decade, was several hundred feet. For future generations, a descent of the *Vallée Blanche* could be by kayak, rather than skis.

For €22, we managed to claim a seat on the train to 'Cham' – we could call it that, since we had now earned our colours. Once there, we celebrated with a beer.

Both Pete and Kathy, mountain guides based in Chamonix, admitted that they had never skied the *Vallée Blanche* in such perfect conditions. It had been exceptional; untracked powder, bluebird skies and hardly anyone around, because the forecast had been so bad.

The *Vallée Blanche* is not the most difficult ski descent in the world, but it has to be among most majestic.

For me, it was one of the best and most memorable day's skiing that I have ever experienced, made even more extraordinary by the once-in-a-lifetime conditions.

18

STRANDED!

You could be stranded in paradise, but you would want to go home eventually!

We were back to the look of reproach from the pups as we left the apartment. Today, we should have listened.

"Take my picture next to that goat." I asked Mark. At the top of Sarezza is a bronze sculpture of an Alpine ibex, *lo stambecco* in Italian. On a less murky day, the Matterhorn would have been visible behind it.

At first, Mark claimed to have lost his phone, then said that he couldn't see anything. Later, I downloaded a photo of some old goat with a big bum in a whiteout. I will leave you to judge how much of me Mark got in frame.

Little did we know that photos were not the only thing that would go horribly wrong today. We arrived in the next valley and the Mandria lift broke down. It was our only route home. We were STRANDED!

I could be stranded on the International Space Station with the lovely, lovely Professor Brian Cox *and* Mr Spock, but I would want to go home eventually... For solid food, if nothing else. And gravity.

We were nowhere near the International Space Station or its sexy, raven-haired scientists, and I am not sure that Mark would have been terribly interested if we were. Solid food was definitely an option, however; we consoled ourselves with *strudel* and a few too many coffees in one of the mountain huts. As far as gravity went, we would experience mixed feelings about that later. After a couple of hours, the lift remained resolutely immobile. We were worried. We had puppies to get back to...

Sometimes, the only way to reach the light at the end of the tunnel is to stomp down there and switch it on yourself. With skis strapped to our backpacks, we set off to walk up the red piste to the Bettaforca lift. Our only other option was a long and expensive taxi ride all the way down the Champoluc valley, then back up the Gressoney valley to Staffal.

They dropped like flies. Fit, young boys just fell by the wayside. Then to add insult to injury, the indolent laggards who had failed to take charge of their own destiny came past, whooping encouragement at us.

Abe Lincoln said, "Good things come to those who wait, but only what's left from those who hustle." Here was a bunch of failed hustlers who had been rewarded lavishly for waiting feebly by the lift or coiffing *vin chaud* in the restaurant. They waved at us as though we should be delighted that they were being borne effortlessly up the slope aboard a *Pisten Bully* piste machine.

It wasn't only the shameless glee of all the lazybones getting a free ride as we slogged uphill in ski boots, carrying our skis and gasping for breath like a bunch of beached goldfish in the thin air.

I wanted a go on a piste machine!

Forty-five minutes into our hike, just as we were in sight of our destination, the Bettaforca lift, the *Pisten Bully* came back to pick us up. You could say that it took us the whole nine yards (well, about fifty, anyhow, but I suppose every little helps.)

It reminded me very much of the time Mark's boom clamp broke about half a mile off shore, rendering his sail ineffective. He spent forty minutes swimming back to shore with his windsurfer in tow. Just as he got his feet down and stood up, exhausted, about ten yards from the beach, the lifeguard (who had been watching him for at least the last half hour) heroically leapt in to save him.

Still, a bad day skiing is better than a good day in the office. And this wasn't even a bad day – just a new (and rather tiring) experience.

As some of our skiing friends pointed out, it was about time we got ourselves some touring bindings and skins.

Skins, originally seal skins, fit to the bottom of your skis. They slide when pushed forward but grip when pushed backwards, so they allow you to walk uphill on your skis.

Once you remove the skins, you ski downhill as normal. Touring boots have a 'walk' setting and the bindings release from the ski at the heel to make walking easier. This set-up allows powder hounds and ski tourers to 'skin' into remote areas of the back country to find the holy grail of untracked powder.

19

LOST! AN UNEXPECTED ADVENTURE

A Cautionary Tale About Earning Your Turns

The Urban Dictionary defines an 'Oh Shit' moment as 'The point in time when you realise that what you originally thought was a good idea, was in actuality, really stupid.'

Everything was perfect – a beautiful, sunny day, snow like icing sugar, an exhilarating descent on the Del Colle piste from Bettaforca. Following a blizzard, the powder at the side of the slope looked too inviting. It was not steep, we knew that it was safe from avalanches – and we'd been that way before with a guide. Except that we hadn't...

We floated along through the trees, drinking in the sun-drenched views as we glided on a gentle incline past the stone houses in deserted summer villages. There were cliffs further on, but we were nowhere near them. Shortly, we would cross a little bridge and rejoin the main slope, since our line of descent was parallel to the piste. Except that it wasn't...

Maybe it was when we avoided a dip and chose the high ground to the right. We're not sure, but somewhere along the way, we got off track.

In the brevity of the moment that it took the unyielding granite walls to block out the sun, the carefree atmosphere evaporated. The gentle, open, powder slope transformed into a shadowy, narrow path of ice, holes and jutting rocks as we entered the couloir. The gulley curved away, concealing what lay ahead. I noticed heavy accumulations of snow above; an avalanche risk that could easily bury an unwary skier very deeply in the terrain trap of a canyon. And somewhere indeterminate beyond, we knew there were cliffs.

It was one of those moments when you think, "If only I hadn't got out of bed this morning..."

Our fur babies were waiting for us to return. Going off-piste today had been a spontaneous decision. Although we always carry our shovels, probes and avalanche transceivers, we were only skiing on the side of the slope, so we hadn't prepared fully or taken any of our usual precautions.

The full horror of our situation began to unfold. No-one knew where we were; we didn't know where we were – and we didn't know how to get out. We had no idea what lay further along the couloir; whether it got more extreme or ended in a precipice. I knew that we weren't near *Disney Channel* – an extreme off-piste descent, which incorporates a forty-metre abseil midway, but already, it was too steep to walk out where we had skied in.

"We will have to climb out here, before the walls get too sheer." Mark said. "There's no way of knowing what's further on and we haven't brought ropes, so if it ends in a cliff, we'll be really stuck."

The climb out was quite an undertaking. Tears of grief and true terror pricked my eyes as I watched Mark clamber up the sides. He was forced to remove his skis and push them upright into the snow, to use the tips as hand holds. All the while, I prayed that the slope would not give way and throw him down into the rocky couloir. The fall would surely kill him. If it didn't, in such a confined space, he would be buried deeply beneath avalanche debris, leaving me a quarter of an hour to find him and dig him out. All I could do was look on and feel helpless.

After an eternity, Mark reached the trees at the top of the wall and snow slope. He grabbed one to stabilise himself, then I followed in his tracks, exposing myself to the same risks. I thrashed through the thick snow and hauled myself the twenty feet or so out of the couloir; my skis gave me the advantage of two additional hand holds. Mark laughed with relief and made light of things when I reached the top. Unlike me, it didn't seem to have occurred to him at any point that we might die.

We skied on through the trees in deep powder, finding no sign of the piste. On any other day, a descent such as this would have been sheer bliss. In the circumstances, it brought no joy – only fear that we were getting further off track.

A right-handed turn brought us to the bottom of the couloir – it didn't end in a cliff. As we looked back up from the other side of the bend, we saw that we could have skied it easily. However, not knowing what lay in store, we had made the correct decision.

Eventually, we found a marked snow-shoe track and came upon a road.

"I am sure that will go to Frachey. From there, we can get the train up to the Mandria lift." I said.

"What if it doesn't?" Mark replied.

So, we slogged up the track, herring-boning and side-stepping hundreds of feet uphill on our skis. It was exhausting, but later, when we looked on the map, we saw that Mark was right. Following the road down would have taken us still further into the wilderness.

The top opened out into a car park near the Mandria ski lift. We collapsed in relief before pulling ourselves together to slog across to the mountain refuge Lo Retsignon for fortification. As suddenly as we had got off track, we found ourselves back in civilisation. We were no longer lost in the snow – and we hadn't fallen down a cliff. People who had spent the morning in the cosseted world of groomed slopes and piste patrol looked askance at our shocked faces as we sipped our hot chocolate. They could have no idea of the ordeal we had just endured.

We had set out to find untracked powder and

untracked powder we found, but it was a cautionary tale.

Off-piste skiers know that they must earn their turns, but on this occasion, we had almost paid too much.

20

WINTER WALKIES – COUMARIAL & ORESTES HÜTTE

The Italian Scots, A Spinone Tow & A Black Bundle in a Backpack

Let me introduce Caroline and Graham – The Smiths. They are two lovely friends that we didn't know we had, until they joined us for the season in Gressoney.

They came with, Oscar, a *Spinone Italiano*. Oscar is a handsome and imposing dog, with a wiry, liver and white coat. Although we could easily express his height in hands, his nature is gentle and laid back. And if you massage his paws, he's yours forever.

Before Gressoney, we had never met The Smiths. Tales of fun in a little gem of an Italian resort, filtered back via a mutual friend, had proved irresistible. Thankfully, we all get on famously – including the pooches. Caroline and Graham are delightful company, although there remains one bone of contention between us. While we are known throughout the valley as 'That couple with four dogs', they operate under the simple handle, 'Oscarrrr!' The handsome hound attracts attention wherever he goes and is the only furbie who upstages our cute, fluffy pack.

Our little minx, Lani, fell head over paws for Oscar.

Lani weighs only six kilos, but doesn't seem to appreciate that she is small. She befriends every canine behemoth that we meet, which is occasionally quite alarming. With no filter regarding friend or foe, Lani bowls up to any bristling creature, whose fangs are dripping blood, to roll over and show her tummy. In front of beasts renowned for their intolerance and fiery tempers, such as the Romanian shepherd dogs encountered on our travels, she will dash in and out like a *Blitzkrieger* to deliver a swift kiss on the nose.

Lani's ability to charm reminds me of my friend Bruce. A freelancer with a passion for travel to remote places, Bruce would drop off the radar every now and then. His trips included activities such as trekking alone through places like Afghanistan in the 1990s, during the Mujahideen guerrilla / Taliban phase. Brucie inevitably reappeared months later with disturbing holiday snaps showing him grinning beneath his towering backpack. Usually, his arms would be draped over the shoulders of armed militia, sporting bandoliers of bullets across their chests.

"They were really nice blokes!" he explained in his cut-glass accent. "And the mountains were lovely."

Any normal person doing the same would be taken

hostage or executed. As with Lani, something about Bruce's innocence and guilelessness enabled him to get away with it.

Anyway, I digress. With Caroline, Graham and Oscar, we discovered some beautiful walks. Two firm favourites were Coumarial and Orestes Hütte.

A forty-five minute drive from Staffal, above Fontainemore, is the gorgeous, remote area of Coumarial, at the foot of the Mont Mars Nature Reserve. High in the mountains on the eastern side of the Gressoney valley, Coumarial is very pleasant in winter, since it keeps the sun for much of the afternoon. There, we found miles of groomed snow shoe and cross-country skiing circuits, with rapturous views at every turn. A mountain hut next to the car park provides refreshments, but the best thing to do is wait for nice weather and take a picnic.

It always makes me smile when people ask why we want to spend the winter months somewhere cold. There might be snow on the ground, but when the sun shines, most of our puppy-walking and terrace time is spent in T-Shirts. I am not sure that people believe us, but Monte Rosa is exceptionally sunny. In our first three-month season, we had barely seven individual days which did not boast blue skies. A local whom we met at Coumarial explained why,

"The prevailing weather comes from the west. Chamonix and Mont Blanc get the worst of it, while Monte Rosa usually basks in sunshine."

The first time we walked to Orestes Hütte was on Valentine's Day. From the Gabiet gondola, we joined the off-piste traverse, which forms the exit for the Indren ski itineraries. Since we were walking towards oncoming skiers, it was easy to step to the side to let them pass. The path was well skied, so we presumed that it would be firm enough to walk on. Mostly it was – although there were places where we sank up to our hips in soft snow. All part of the adventure!

The initial section of the route sneaks under an imposing cliff. Down a vertiginous slope to our left, we saw a frozen cascade in the valley below, where the river Endre pours over a drop. When Mark and I first skied this traverse, it scared us. Although we now have the skills to control our speed on such bumpy, icy paths, we retain our respect for the environment. However, this walk treated us to a checklist of the potential misfortunes that lie in wait off-piste if you don't take navigation seriously.

"Three skiers went over that waterfall. That was a helicopter rescue!" was one tale that we heard on the Gabiet gondola.

As we crossed above, we got a great view of the entrance to the canyon, *Leisch*, or 'Middle Earth' that we had skied with Richard. There, a most incongruous sight greeted us; half a dozen Italian skiers and snow-boarders, wearing kilts and red wigs, topped with Tam-o'-Shanter hats. (We knew that they were Italian because we met them later. As I will explain, we were pleased to see them.)

The *Scozzese Italiani* had made the schoolboy error of dropping too low to join the traverse out of the Endre valley. They were trying to clamber a hundred feet back up the impossibly steep slope to where we were standing. Their only other option was the gnarly descent through *Leisch*.

"*Leisch* is in good condition," the person on the gondola had said. "The rocks are all covered because it's recently filled up with avalanche snow." Such a description should send every off-pister's panic radar into overdrive. None of the kilted contingent had backpacks, so they had no avalanche rescue kit – and a kilt is not ideal to keep you warm if you're lost or stuck in the snow.

Further on, past the convex slope where Dave had pointed out the surface hoar, the valley opened out into the Endre basin. There, we met a real Scotsman skiing with his young son. Hamish had only a piste map to guide him on his off-piste itinerary. He smoothed it out and asked,

"Wheer's the way oot?"

We pointed him in the right direction and urged him to keep high, to avoid joining the Kilt club's climbing convention.

It took us just over an hour to walk the couple of kilometres from Gabiet to Orestes. The ascent is approximately three-hundred metres (one-thousand-feet) on an even gradient, until the last section. That is properly steep – and you have to avoid the hazard of skiers travelling down it at the speed of light. Like me, they don't want to pole along the flat bit.

Graham kindly offered Oscar's services to me for the final quarter of a mile. I grabbed Oscar's harness – and have to say that the Spinone tow was most welcome. It was certainly a lot more sedate than the horse-tow in the Dolomites.

A trip to Orestes is always special. My very first visit had been on my birthday several years previously. Then, Dave, the mountain guide, had even got me cake and a candle. I suppose that if you must come to terms with birthdays getting higher, you might as well do it properly – so I hit 2,600 metres.

Our lunch on the sunny terrace was a chilled and relaxed affair. Keeping The Fab Four, Oscar and The Boss separate was easy, since the magnificent feline only patrols indoors. While the wonderful food and stunning location tempted us to stay, we knew that at some point in the early afternoon, we would lose the sun behind the mountain.

Sunlight still caressed the marked snow-shoe track that we followed across the combe to return to the Gabiet gondola. When we looked back, we could see Orestes Hütte cloaked in shadow. I am not sure whether her paws got chilly or she just fancied a rest, but part way down, Lani asked us to pick her up. Caroline and I giggled as we stuffed her into Mark's backpack. She seemed to love riding high and looking out over his shoulder. For the next few days, it took a little persuasion to convince her that when we went out, it was for walkies, not carries!

The terrace of the Adler Nest refuge, just above the Gabiet lift station, was still bathed in sun, so we stopped for a final coffee. We needed sustenance for our ride home in the gondola, high above the Moos valley. At the bus stop in Staffal, we saw the *Scozzese Italiani* again. It was a relief to see them safe, although I had to avert my eyes when they all bent over to take off their skis.

Decorum dictates that I can't let you into the secret of what Italian Scotsmen wear under their kilts.

21

THERE'S NO BUSINESS LIKE SNOW BUSINESS – OUR SEASON IN THE ALPS!

Musings on our Months in The Mountains

Three months into our stay in Monte Rosa, we had really got into the swing of things. We loved the ever-changing views of the mountains, the smell of log fires and the muffled silence of a snow-covered wilderness. The days had been a glorious blur of joyous ski descents and beautiful walks with the dogs under bluebird skies, followed by a sauna, a simple, hearty meal and a D.V.D.

Our skiing had improved markedly, although the only Italian that I could claim to have learnt is *emorroidi* – the word for haemorrhoids. This is a condition from which the Italian version of *Facebook* seemed to think I suffered, judging by the frequency of pop-up ads for some special kind of haemorrhoid-relieving toilet paper.

I had wondered whether the dogs might affect our

enjoyment of the skiing, but winter walking added another dimension. What we had done most days with our little pack was true back-country. We rarely saw a soul; I enjoyed the afternoon walks every bit as much as our morning ski.

The dogs loved the snow more than we could have hoped. Each morning, Rosie was up with the larks and cried to go out to play. If crying failed to gird her tired humans into action, she had worked out how to flick the curtains to create an impressive stroboscopic light show to raise us from our slumber. Whenever we called her back inside from the garden, she shuffled like a reluctant teenager. Distracted by anything and everything, she would shamble resentfully to the door.

"Oooh look! A lump of ice."

"Gosh! Would you believe it? I've just found some snow!"

"I'm coming, but there's this *fascinating* icicle to sniff…"

All the pups enjoyed gnawing the copious little larch cones when we walked through the trees. Many of these half-chewed cones found their way into our bed, along with balls of snow, which they loved to chase and then bring home to eat as an iced treat.

Rosie was definitely the downhill racer. She thrives on excitement and thoroughly embraced the thrill of bounding down an incline to gain momentum. Lani and Ruby are The Powder Hounds. They both used their spaniel bounce to propel themselves kangaroo-like through powder snow. Poor Kai simply had to master how to get up again out of the deep drifts when bowled over by a hyper-accelerated Rosie, as she hit him frequently like a bullet from above.

The pooches made friends with much of the canine community in Gressoney. Red, a little dog from around the corner, popped in to see the pack most days. A pair of ears and a nose appearing at the window to a cacophony of barking heralded the arrival of the elderly Alsatian from down the road in Cimavalle, whom we met on one of our very first walks.

Socially, we had not been inactive. Besides the friendly Russians in the sauna, we encountered most of the U.K.'s windsurfing community on the gondolas, in addition to a chap who went to school in my home town. While Svetlana and Artur worked on persuading us to go to Moscow or St Petersburg, I learned from a friend that there is a History of the Toilet Museum in Kyiv. I am not sure about the practicalities of caravanning in Russia and the Ukraine. Nevertheless, a Toilet Museum has an inescapable allure to someone who planned a whole holiday around an Umbrella Museum in Stresa that she read about in her Italian language textbook.

And a History of the Toilet Museum would surely be the place to discover everything I need to know about haemorrhoid-relieving toilet paper.

22
SPRING IS COMING TO THE MOUNTAINS!

We Encounter the Snowy Equivalent of Antimatter

By way of recovery from our various adventures, we sat on the sun terrace with our fur babies. A Polish family came along and told us to go to Hel.

Their daughter had come over from the bar next door to fuss the dogs. Conversation eventually led to our lifestyle and travels. When they discovered our plan to visit Poland, they said,

"You must go to Hel. It is one of the best windsurfing spots in Poland!"

Our focus was beginning to move from skiing to future travel plans because spring was coming to the mountains. A bank that was buried under half a metre of snow the previous week was now resplendent with dainty white crocuses, plus a single, purple bloom. In the woods, until recently scentless and crystallised, we sucked in the luscious, resinous aroma of pine. The snow-muffled silence of the valley had given way to the trill of birdsong. Their sweet melody overlaid a background of the rushing waters of the River Lys; now a torrent, not a stream, as she filled with meltwater.

As far as skiing went, we got out our ski gear and propped the skis against the doorway. Then we sat in the sun and Ruby jumped on to my lap for a cuddle. One of our house rules is that if you are cuddling a dog, you are exempt from all tasks and can't move until the dog gets up of its own accord.

Ruby stayed put and after Mark brought me several cups of tea, a bunch of British *Saisonnières* from Champoluc joined us. Then the waitress came over to say,

"A small dog called Kalynka is coming to see you at three o'clock."

When we looked confused, she giggled and said, "My English is not very good!"

Intrigued, we waited and the penny dropped when our new, seven-year-old Polish friend, Kalina, made a return visit with her lovely family to play with the dogs. So, we never did quite go skiing.

The following day dawned with perfect blue sky. Again. However, by now, The Fab Four had worked out a fool proof system to prevent or delay our departure to ski. They would cuddle, or blockade the door, or look up at us with sad eyes... Sometimes, they would even do all three.

But we are brutal puppy parents, so we did it. We left them to go skiing. In a rare moment, Mark and I were within a kilometre of each other, but I'm afraid that I had finally lost him. I could no longer keep up.

And then it snowed. For over twenty-four hours. The avalanche risk moved to 4 ('High') with zero visibility. Nevertheless, the pull of potential POW persuaded us to venture forth. Instead, we encountered the snowy equivalent of antimatter. Coming into contact with matter (our skis) it consumed them.

"This is not champagne powder!" I complained to Mark as we wallowed and sank in snow the consistency of porridge.

As we skied through the trees near Mandria, we passed a lady instructor as we popped back on to the piste. Our thighs were burning with the effort of pushing through the liquid concrete. She looked at us and, as if reading our thoughts, she concurred,

"It is 'orrible!"

I tweaked my good knee trying to turn in it. Mark hurt his good shoulder when his ski hit a rock and launched him out of the front door. After so much snow, we had considered extending our stay for another week. Now, our minds were made up beyond doubt. As we ploughed our way home in rain – RAIN – we heard a deep, low rumble that sounded like a jet engine. We saw the avalanche as it plunged down the flanks of Telcio, the mountain behind our residence. It was clear. Our season was over.

We took our skis in for storage wax and brought forward our Channel Tunnel crossing.

It was our last drive along our magical valley before

leaving. There were so many waterfalls; no longer frozen, they cascaded down the mountainsides for hundreds if not thousands of feet. Back in the U.K., each would be a tourist attraction. They dwarfed the likes of Swallow Falls or Aira Force. We stopped in Gressoney St Jean for one final walk on the banks of the river Lys.

Gressoney St Jean has its own Weissmatten ski area, which is separate from the main Monte Rosa pistes. The black run, named in memory of local skier Leonardo David, was recently voted 'the most beautiful ski run in Italy'. The bottom part is floodlit, which presents night-skiing opportunities, but we had not skied it. Being lower down the valley, the snow had not been great.

High above us, we could see the Walser settlement of Alpenzu Grande just on the snow line. It was inhabited year-round until the beginning of the 20th century – although I wouldn't mind inhabiting its lofty lodges now.

Earlier in the season, we had tried to walk up to Alpenzu. Accessible only via a precipitous mule track, adjacent to a magnificent, frozen waterfall, we had struggled on the icy steps. When we saw a man descending in crampons, we thought it wise to abandon our attempt. Subsequently, we didn't get around to trying again.

So, there was no choice. Next year, we would need to come back. We still had things to do.

23

SLOPING OFF

The Art of Conversation; Grandma's Advice on the Maintenance of Marital Bliss & Cracking Codes...

Mark and I are 'differently organised'. It caused a last-minute panic.

"I can't find the lead for the satnav!" he moaned.

I like to keep related things together; like satnav and satnav lead. Mark likes to keep related things together; like leads. Hundreds of them. Wound like spaghetti in a homogenous and undifferentiated mass; intertwined and squirming like a scary nest of vipers. And all buried somewhere in the back of a fully loaded van...

It was departure day from our three-month stay in Staffal. We had a long drive ahead; from the Alps to the U.K. This was not your dream beginning.

A full empty and re-load of the van solved the crisis. Ready for the off, Mark asked,

"What are the details of tonight's hotel?"

"I don't know. It's written in the diary."

"Where's the diary...?"

Crisis resumed...

They say that, 'A journey of a thousand miles starts with a single step.' However, for us, our journey of thousand miles started with two complete empty-and-reloads of Big Blue.

Despite this mega faff, we still hit the road more-or-less on schedule at 9:30am.

Monte Rosa's last smile was a clear, cornflower-blue sky pierced by the peak of St Anna, rising like a three-thousand metre bride. Shyly, she sported the full skirts of an immense, virginal-white wedding dress.

But the mountains' palette was changing. Stark, winter white against the backdrop of a cloudless, azure sky was giving way to a wave of bright Alpine green. A verdant blanket was creeping back up the valley, reclaiming the territory stolen by the wintry fingers of frost.

As we descended, we passed a fresh bank of primroses. Blossom trees danced and waved farewell from the gardens of stone houses. Tiny crystals of mica shone gold in the stone, fish-scale roof tiles, absorbing the sun, now that they had shed their blankets of snow.

The valley looked as though an exuberant three-year-old had gone wild with a set of dayglo felt-tipped pens. Everything white had been coloured in. To underline the change, as we dropped into Pont St Martin, a carpet of pink camellia petals flew up around the van like confetti. Even the austere hilltop fortresses that guarded Pont St Martin were softening into spring.

Away from the treacherous mountain roads, we eased up to an 80mph cruise on the *autostrada*. Other than on skis, we realised that this was the fastest we had travelled for three months.

By midday, we were enjoying our traditional coffee beneath the *Aiguille du Midi*, watching the tiny dot of the cable car rise steeply to the jagged peak. The menacing glaciers of Mont Blanc glistened impenetrably in the sunlight, the mountain's shining, armoured breastplate. A few miles on, we saw the sign for *Le Pont Percée*; a mountain with a hole in it up ahead. Mark spotted the actual hole, but I couldn't see it.

"That's a shame," he teased, "because it's the *best* thing I have *ever* seen in my life!"

So, it was going to be like that.

One thing that attracted me to Mark was his knowledge of codes, which actually surpassed my own. I considered myself quite unique. For many years, I managed a sales territory which extended from Plymouth to Hull. This gave me a spectacularly comprehensive insight into English postcodes and telephone dialling codes. For no reason other than sheer fascination, I am also well acquainted with the meaning behind vehicle registration numbers.

As a former logistics manager, Mark truly delivered. He brought Scottish postcodes, country identification codes and I.A.T.A. three-letter airport codes into this marriage. I love him for it. It helps to atone for the sarcasm, at any rate.

My Grandma, born in the early 1900s, once spoke to me sagely about how to create a successful marriage.

"*All that business,*" as she called it, "might take up an hour. What will you and your husband do for the other twenty-three?"

As Big Blue ate up the miles, we answered the twenty-three-hour question. Along the *autoroute*, we observed a vast cornucopia of international number plates. When we reached the *Services Poulet de Bresse*, (advertised by a giant, wire chicken) we had been through the country codes of every E.U. country, from Austria (A) to Turkey (TR). *(I appreciate that Turkey's not, yet, at any rate, but my criteria for entry are more relaxed than the E.U.'s. We allowed Turkey in because we saw a Turkish lorry – and alphabetically, TR is the closest we got to Z.)*

It was all getting a bit hysterical by then, so I threw a curve ball to challenge Mark's expertise.

"What is the country code for B'diddly Boing Oda Idaho?"

He didn't know. When I cleverly postulated that, "It must be BD", he got started on postcodes.

"BD is Bradford. What is the postcode for Birmingham?"

"B".

We shot through postcodes for towns beginning

with B. To keep things interesting, he changed format with the letter C.

"What is CA?"

"Carlisle."

"What is CB?"

"Cambridge"

How the time flew!

So much so that I confidently asserted that there was nowhere answering to the postcode CR. This turned out to be a little embarrassing. CR is Croydon. Not memorable to most people, but Croydon is the town where I joined the club *Spice*, which changed my life in many ways – including the introduction to my husband. It is where I set up my own business. Had my office. And lived for several years...

An interesting fact; CDQ is the three-letter code for Croydon Airport, Australia. You may not know but the U.K.'s Croydon Airport has its place in aviation history. Amy Johnson, Charles Lindbergh and Winston Churchill all flew from Croydon. Before Heathrow, Croydon was the U.K.'s main international airport.

I begged Mark to stop at CZ, which is not a postcode, but the country code for The Czech Republic. I figured that it was time to change the subject.

We passed a lorry that said, *Nous Aimons la Verre*.

"We Love Glass," I translated. "Did you know that glass is a supercooled fluid?"

"I think I did..."

"Ha! You've forgotten!"

After nearly twenty years of marriage, we have

explored most topics of conversation. In our case, those themes extend to encompass fluid dynamics and other random subjects. These are usually heralded by Mark's heart sinking as I utter the words "I know an interesting fact..."

Mark was obviously in need of a refresher.

"Medieval panes of glass are thicker at the bottom because glass is actually a fluid that flows gradually downwards over time. What is a thixotropic fluid?"

"Tomato ketchup."

"You *remembered* that one! Define a thixotropic fluid?"

"Tomato ketchup."

"No – what are the *properties* of a thixotropic fluid?"

He mumbled something about viscosity. Over to me.

"It's when you have to apply shock for it to flow. Like having to bang the bottom of a sauce bottle or shake it to make the sauce come out."

"Or squeeze it," he replied.

"That's not strictly true. *Jif Lemon* isn't thixotropic and you can squeeze that."

"But it still makes it come out of the bottle."

"Yes, but it's not thixotropic."

"But that's not my point. I am *not* making a point about it being thixotropic. My point is that if you squeeze it, it still comes out of the bottle."

I warned you that it was going to be like that.

I had to concede. Further wise words imparted by my Grandma were that,

"Sometimes, the best way to win is to forget to keep score."

We stopped for forty minutes at the *Aire Pont Val de Saône* for the dogs to stretch their legs in a beautiful, shady copse, carpeted with daisies and wood anemones. With Rosie and Kai chasing the ball through fallen leaves, Ruby got an unexpected variant of The Leaf Kicking Game that she so loves in autumn. She followed along and snapped at their trails of flying leaves. While we can't be sure, we believe that this interlude may subsequently have come back to haunt us in the form of a virulent tummy bug and a substantial vet's bill.

As we continued our drive, we passed a Swiss car and realised; we'd forgotten to name the country code for Switzerland. Spain's 'E' derives from *España* and Germany's 'D' comes from *Deutschland*; but CH – "What does it stand for?"

After a short cogitation, we decided it must be **CH**ocolate. What a subject.

"The triangles in Toblerones are more widely spaced these days. It means less chocolate in the Toblerone."

We pursued the issue right through the contraction of the *Curly Wurly*, miniaturisation of *Mars Bars* – and what about *Wagon Wheels*? C'mon. They used to be HUGE!

On tour, they say it's not the destination that matters, but the journey. It must be because of the conversation. (Although our friend John said that he loves travelling with his girlfriend, because as soon as they get in the car, she opens her *Kindle* and that's the last he hears from her...)

And so, we returned to civilisation, if you could call it that. Our overnight stop was a budget hotel on an industrial estate in Troyes. Right on the junction of the D610 and D619, vast, furniture warehouses and a *Leclerc* supermarket the size of Berkshire surrounded us. Our room enjoyed a view of both *McDonald's* and a *Burger King* opposite.

It was a struggle to adjust. We had grown accustomed to the tiny village shop, which was rarely open and never had what you wanted when it was. With hindsight, this was beneficial, since a small pack of frozen peas required a bank loan. The budget hotel charged us €4 per dog – the going rate for a meagre, plastic pouch of frozen peas in Staffal.

The pooches had all been bathed and, except for Lani, smelt of almond shampoo. Our little malodorous minx had somehow assumed the aroma of a sweaty trainer by doing nothing more than sitting in Big Blue. Lani has an amazing ability to assume odours. Some, like manure and fox poo, are easily explained by her penchant for rolling. The spontaneous appearance of scents, such as curry behind her ears when she has done nothing but play in the snow, still perplex us.

It was a lovely, warm evening, so we decided to push the boat out, treat ourselves and dine out. I took a seat in the sunshine outside *McDonald's* while Mark went inside to order the food. As I admired the industrial estate, a family approached. Freshly shampooed pups clearly maintained their appeal. I heard the words "*veux*" (want) and "*chien*" (dog). Having not quite understood, I started a guessing game in French.

"Do you want to stroke the dogs?" The look of horror registered on the children's faces answered that one.

The man pointed at Lani. "You want the dog?" Furious head shaking...

Suddenly, it all became clear. "You want to *give* me a dog?"

Clearly, since we had four, they thought we might not notice another. I had to explain,

"We're travelling to England tomorrow and the dogs need passports."

Luckily, the dog was not with them. A dog in need of rescue – I might have wavered. (We returned from Romania with an extra dog; a Transylvanian stray, now happily re-homed with friends.)

I know you get a free toy with a *McDonald's Happy Meal*, but I have never been offered a free dog.

24

PISTE OFF BACK IN BLIGHTY

The Art of Avoiding Morning Coffee, Conversation & Brexit

"Where's the diary? It's got the postcode for the Channel Tunnel in it."

As it had the previous day, disorder delayed our departure. I mentioned that Mark and I are differently organised. I am not the tidiest person, but when I do put things away, they mostly end up somewhere sensible, if not in their proper place. Mark, on the other hand, just likes things to be away. And this is, of course, why we eventually found the diary in the food bag.

Destination co-ordinates entered, we emerged from the Nirvana of our industrial estate to a broad, agricultural landscape, punctuated by regimented lines of poplar trees and wind turbines, all mysterious in a pink, morning mist. It seemed very French.

Something else mysterious and very French was *McDonalds* being closed at 7:49am. A sign on the door announced that the *Glace* machine had broken, so even if they had been open, a *McFlurry* was out of the question. The first motorway service station that we passed was also *fermé*.

"What do you have to do to get your morning coffee in France?" we wondered.

As we drove, as a digression from the country codes, postcodes and fluid dynamics explored in conversation yesterday, Mark tested me on my Baltic Capitals;

1. Lithuania – Vilnius
2. Estonia – Tallinn
3. Latvia – Riga.

Our musings took us on to whether Brexit would trigger a repeal the E.U. colour coding on fire extinguishers. We agreed that the old British system of different coloured fire extinguishers to correlate with the different types of fire was definitely superior to having them all red, with just a small, coloured label.

A friend of mine, Jan, once gave a stranger a lift to a *Spice* event a few hours' drive away. His conversation bored her so much that it forced Jan, a lovely polite girl, to suggest that the only way things would work was if he didn't speak for the rest of the journey.

It was still a three-hour drive to reach the Channel Tunnel. In silent and tacit agreement, Mark and I opted to switch on some music.

By 9am, we were in Champagne and had our worst

and most expensive coffee to date. €7.20 for two *Latte Macchiati* made with powdered milk, and,

"No, you can't sell me a croissant for €5."

We had bought four delicious, fresh ones from the bakery in *Leclerc's* for €1.20.

Reckless expenditure at this level did not bode well for my reduction and reassignment of the coffee budget into the alcohol budget to atone for my new pair of skis, recently purchased in the end of season sale.

For Mark and I, there are only two seasons; Skiing and Caravan.

When we arrived back in Blighty, it was the warmest March day since 2012. After her first winter storage, I was thrilled and relieved that when we collected her, Caravan Kismet was condensation-free and didn't smell of mould. In fact, she smelt pleasingly like a new van. I smugly self-congratulated on my silica-gel-kitty-litter-spread-around-in-*Tupperwares* as a solution to keeping things dry over winter. (Kitty litter in a pop sock is also a great way to dry and de-odourise boots and ski gloves.)

Despite dire warnings about the preparations required for over-wintering, other than a mouldy plastic tube (the one we use to fill the *Aquaroll* water container) and a brief splutter of reluctance from the

Whale water pump, everything was still fully functional. Or so we thought.

We enjoyed our First Supper overlooking a lake and listening to the birds – we were so happy to be back in the caravan. The pups chased around on the woodland dog walk immediately next to our pitch. Since there were squirrels to keep them occupied, they did not miss the snow

Unlike our last homecoming, it thrilled us not to return to an array of outstanding fines and, having been away for three months, a court summons for non-payment of said fines. Foolishly, we thought everything was going swimmingly, but our homecomings are never straightforward.

On April 1st, Ruby became very ill. We could not be sure of the cause; The Fab Four had all played in the leaves in the motorway services in France. Since it was an area probably frequented by other dogs, it may have been an infection – or the old, autumn leaves could have had mould on them, which can be very toxic to dogs. It is also possible that the illness was an adverse reaction to the tapeworm treatment administered just before we left, as required by the U.K. Pet Passport regulations. Although the £320 vet bill was an unwelcome blow to the budget, the fact that she made a full and swift recovery made it worth every penny.

Then, a trip to our dealer to investigate Kismet's water ingress problem for a second time did not end well. The water had entered through a large hole, caused by the offside tyre rubbing against the wheel arch. Despite being a sprightly two-year-old, the cause was the collapse of Kismet's axle. Even better, the dealer added,

"It's not covered under warranty because it's your own fault. Your caravan is overloaded."

This was a difficult accusation to take. Our friends refer to us as The Compulsive Obsessives because we have a spreadsheet for everything. We produced the 'Caravan Weight' one and gave it to the dealer. It showed that we had weighed every item of the caravan's contents, including teaspoons, on a calibrated scale. This time- and date-stamped evidence was confirmation that the weight of the contents did not exceed the payload.

In addition, we produced Section 3.5 of The D.V.S.A. (Driver and Vehicle Standards Agency) 'Code of Practice for the enforcement weighing of vehicles.' This demonstrated that the overload of which they accused us fell within the error margins of their portable weighbridge. They told us that they had never heard of the D.V.S.A. 'Code of Practice for the enforcement weighing of vehicles.' As such, it didn't surprise us that they never did produce a certificate to prove that they had calibrated their weighbridge according to the specified procedures.

Faced with evidence and some rules from an official body, the dealer grudgingly replaced our axle free of charge. It meant that we were homeless for a month, sofa surfing with friends and family, but we used the time wisely. To plan.

Brexit looks likely curb our European travelling lifestyle and is set to transform us into Global Nomads. If freedom of movement ends, the 90/180 Schengen Visa Rule will allow British nationals to spend only ninety days in a rolling one-hundred-and-eighty days (roughly three months in every six) in Europe. This applies not only to the E.U., but the entire Schengen zone, which includes non-E.U. countries such as Iceland, Norway and Switzerland as well. Another season in the Alps would use up half of our year's entitlement. If we used it all at once, it would restrict our ability even to travel through the impenetrable barrier of the E.U. to reach non-Schengen countries. Heavy fines, deportation and a possible ban await those who overstay their welcome.

One alternative would be to remain in the U.K. for three months in the spring, but our mantra is that, "There's always a solution." Our Brexit-Busting tour lies outside the E.U., in places such as Turkey, Georgia, Central Asia and Russia.

"How would you like to go on a road trip and ski in twenty-five different countries? We can ski down Mount Ararat, Mount Olympus and Mount Elbrus."

Married to the skydiving, bungee jumping, White Water Rafting Queen, Mark already knew the answer.

But first, we need to go to Hel.

EPILOGUE

A Dream Descent – 'The Magnificent Seven' Volcanoes, Chile

PENDING.

SO, WHAT DID WE LEARN?

As ever, we have kept our ears to the ground or made the mistakes so you don't have to. Here is a distillation of our best winter holiday advice.

Top Tips for Winter Driving

1. Use low gear, keep your revs high. Apply plenty of power at all times.
2. Wheel spinning increases traction.
3. Wheel spinning with snow chains significantly increases traction.
4. According to one *Facebook* forum, safety equipment, such as winter tyres and snow chains, which are a legal requirement for winter driving in many European countries, constitute 'a frivolous expense'.
5. Using summer tyres in the Alps in winter converts stopping on icy hills, especially at

junctions, into a fabulous game of Russian Roulette. Can you stop? Or will you just slide out straight in front of oncoming traffic?
6. Rear-wheel drive is perfect for icy conditions.
7. A fully laden van with rear-wheel drive is the best of all worlds for driving up mountains in icy conditions.
8. NEVER clear all the snow off your windscreen. Being unable to see where you're going in a hazardous environment adds to the adventure.
9. NEVER clear all the snow off your roof. Other drivers enjoy being hit by snow sloughing off as you move, especially at 80mph on the motorway. It's like a giant snowball fight!
10. People love to be struck by flying gripper tracks. This is most effective when you place them on ice and then wheel spin to increase traction.

Top Tips for Skiing Off Piste

1. Always use narrow carving skis.
2. Hiring or buying the correct safety equipment is a frivolous expense.
3. And carrying it adds weight to your backpack.

4. And if you don't have the correct safety equipment, you don't have to learn how to use it. That is time saved – so more snow time!
5. A kilt and Tam-o'-Shanter is the perfect attire for skiing off-piste.
6. Carving with your ski edges works in all snow conditions, including deep powder, so don't waste time learning new skills.
7. There is no need to check whether your insurance is valid for skiing off piste. The burgeoning U.K. property market means that the sale of your house should cover at least some of the cost of a helicopter rescue.
8. Always ski directly above other groups of skiers. Then, if anyone sets off an avalanche, they get buried and die, not you.
9. It is at odds with Physics, but you can arrest a fall on any slope angle. You will *always* stop at the bottom of the slope, cliff, crevasse – or on the way down if you hit something.
10. You won't need a proper map or compass because bad things, like getting lost or skiing off a precipice, can't happen on holiday.

Top Tips for Making Friends On Piste

1. Carry your skis on your shoulders and turn

around as often as possible. 'The Man With The Plank' gag is always funny – and sharp, metal ski edges at face-level just add to the excitement.

2. While walking with your ski poles, hold them in the centre or near the top, so that as you swing your arms, the pointy ends jab naturally upwards and backwards towards anyone behind. Once you master this, you can poke someone in the eye, then turn around to follow up with 'The Man With The Plank' gag and make it all look inadvertent.

3. People who own their own, expensive skis always appreciate those with hired equipment clambering over their tails in a lift queue. If you can get close enough, you could push them over as well. The slow, twisting fall that is likely in this situation can often result in serious injury, which serves those show-offs right.

4. Barge through the lift queue, then when you're at the gate, stop and wait for your friend. This is most effective if your friend is at least ten people back and at peak times, when there is a massive queue. Everyone behind you will completely understand that it is impossible for you to board the lift without your chum. They will also delight in seeing half-empty chairs rising up the

mountain, thus giving further opportunity for people with hired skis to clamber over their tails.

5. As you alight from a lift, don't move away from the exit before you start faffing with your poles, reading your piste map or waiting for your mates. Watching the pile-up that forms behind you will help pass the time.

6. Snowboarders – make sure to sit right in the middle of the piste, slightly below the sight-line of any blind roller. You will meet lots of people that way and they will immediately become your friend. If a few of you sit in a line right across the piste, you will make even more friends.

7. Big groups – ski really slowly and try to take up the full width of the piste. This will ensure that faster skiers can't get past. For best results, make your turns really unpredictable, so that there is absolutely no opportunity for them to sneak through.

8. If you are in a big group, always stop to re-group on the narrowest part of the piste, preferably just around a blind corner. In the same way as when you are moving, try to occupy as much of the piste as possible. Other slope users enjoy the challenge – being suddenly faced with nowhere to go keeps them on their toes.

9. Nervous beginners LOVE to be buzzed by fast and confident skiers. Get as close as you can and hear them scream their encouragement at you. They can't wait to be as talented as you and scaring them half to death will embolden them and encourage progress.
10. Start your Après early. There is really nothing wrong with being inebriated while shooting down a crowded hill at forty miles per hour. Insurance companies are very understanding of accidents that happen while you are drunk. And if they don't cough up straight away, there is always the burgeoning U.K property market to fall back on.

GLOSSARY

This is a glossary of terms relevant to my book, rather than a comprehensive glossary of terminology for ski geeks, although it is a start if you want to sound knowledgeable in the bar.

European Piste Classification

Ski runs are classified on their steepness, (measured as a percentage grade of slope), width and possibly an indication of how well-groomed they might be. This gives an indication of the degree of difficulty. A steep, narrow slope that is ungroomed is much more difficult to navigate than a perfectly groomed, wide, shallow slope.

Colours are used on piste markers and piste maps to designate the degree of difficulty. Treat it as an indication, rather than an absolute, since it varies from resort to resort. (The grading system in North America, Australia and New Zealand is slightly different from that used in Europe – a rough equivalent is shown below as 'U.S.' classification.)

I still maintain that the toughest bit of piste in Monte Rosa is the short top section of the red run C6 from Sarezza back towards Gressoney. It is steep, narrow, often lumpy or icy – and there are usually a number of bodies to avoid, either on the deck or frozen with terror.

Nursery Slope or **Baby Slope** – A very gentle slope used by small children and absolute beginners to learn to ski.

Green Run – Learner slope. Not all resorts have green pistes; **Blue** often designates the easiest runs.

Blue Run – Beginner slope. In most of Europe, blue indicates the easiest slope, which should have a gradient of less than 25%. *(U.S. – Green Circle.)*

Red Run – Intermediate slope with a gradient less than 40%. *(U.S. – Blue Square.)*

Black Run – Advanced slope. There is no widely-accepted standard, so the pitch of a black run can be anything from easy to O.M.G. Particularly in France, it may or may not be pisted, although in Italy, usually every slope is groomed every night. *(U.S. – Black Diamond: Double- or Triple Black Diamond slopes are even more challenging.)*

Yellow or Orange Slope – Experts only. Also known as *itinéraires*, these are marked off-piste routes, which may not be patrolled or avalanche protected. The markers usually run down the centre of the route, rather than showing the left and right boundaries of the slope. Eagle Couloir in Gressoney has orange markers and is shown on the map as a black dotted line. Zermatt has a 36km network of yellow freeride slopes, which are protected and patrolled but never pisted. There is no standardisation, so in other resorts, such runs may be neither patrolled nor avalanche protected, so always treat them as off-piste and check your insurance.

Types of Snow

It is a myth that the Inuit have over one hundred words for 'snow', although winter sports and winter dog walking do boast quite a few.

Although snow is simply frozen water, it can take many different physical forms. This is as a result of what happens to the snow once it has fallen from the sky.

Recognising different types of snowy surface is helpful both in understanding snow reports and working out the challenge or exultation that they might present to ski. Here are a few of the most common snow types;

Artificial or **Man-Made Snow** – These are essentially tiny particles of ice, created by snow-cannons blowing a fine mist of water into cold air. Snow-making is used to top up natural snow. Artificial snow can feel rougher and stickier to ski on.

Ball Bearings – Hard, icy balls that give you a bone-shaking ride. Larger chunks are known as **Death Cookies.**

Breakable Crust – A frozen top layer with soft snow beneath.

Chop – Soft snow that has been skied and mashed up, but is not solid.

Champagne Powder – The dry, light, beautiful, soft powdery snow that every skier craves – it is the worst for balling up in your dog's fur.

Corduroy – Freshly-groomed snow, whose texture resembles the suit fabric favoured by geography teachers.

Corn Snow – Icy 'ears' or large granules of snow, caused by melting and re-freezing. When softened, it is one of the desirable **Spring Snow** types, but can turn into **Slush** if it gets too warm.

Crud – Heavily skied powder, forming an uneven, bumpy surface comprising a bit of everything.

Crust – A frozen layer either on top of soft snow or buried beneath fresh snow.

Death Cookies – Large chunks of hard snow, often left behind by grooming soft snow, which then freezes into lumps.

Granular – Pellets of ice. **Frozen Granular** is Granular snow which has frozen together. **Loose Granular** is Granular snow broken up by grooming.

Hardpack – Snow that is solid, compressed and dense due to repeated skiing and grooming.

Packed Powder – New-ish snow that is harder than powder because it has been groomed or well skied.

Powder or **POW** – Fresh, dry, light snow. The Holy Grail of skiing and snowboarding.

Sastrugi – Formations created by wind blowing the snow into sharp, ragged ridges.

Slush – Heavy, wet snow as it begins to melt.

Spring Snow – The Goldilocks of snow. Frozen solid in the morning, **Slush** in the afternoon, but a joy if you catch it when it's just right...

Surface Hoar – A layer of moisture from the air that freezes on the surface of the snow overnight, like hoar frost.

Wind Slab – Snow compressed and compacted by wind.

Yellow Snow – Frozen pees!

Glossary of Terms

A

A.B.S Avalanche System – Stands for *Avalanche Balloon Securesystem*. Several companies offer similar avalanche airbag systems, which work on the principle that larger items rise to the top in an avalanche. They all deploy single or multiple air bags from a backpack, which inflate when the skier pulls a cord. (Some models can be activated remotely by other group members.) Most use gas from a cartridge, although some use a rechargeable, battery-powered fan.

All-Mountain or **All-Terrain Skis** – Skis that are wider underfoot than **Carving Skis** (usually from 85 to 105mm) and can handle a variety of conditions on and off-piste.

Alpine Skiing – Sliding downhill on snow with a pair of planks strapped to your feet.

Après-Ski – Finishing off your day on the slopes. Usually involves consuming buckets of beer and/or downing shots (*Jägermeister* is popular with snowboarders and the young) – then bragging about your exploits and dancing on the tables to Europop in ski boots. The footwear aspect is much easier if you're a snowboarder.

Avalanche Beacon – Also known as a **Transceiver**, this safety device is worn by sensible snow sports people when they venture off-piste. It transmits a signal to enable rescuers armed with transceivers to locate them should they be buried by an avalanche.

Avalanche Probe – A telescopic pole, which a searcher pokes through avalanche debris to physically locate a buried victim.

Avalanche Shovel – A spade used to dig out the buried victim – metal is best.

B

Back-Country – The back-country is the **Freeride** or **Off-Piste** area well away from the lifts and marked ski slopes. It is not marked, patrolled or protected against avalanche dangers and the rider will be faced with all kinds of natural, un-groomed snow and terrain.

Basket – The round or star-shaped disc on the bottom of a ski pole, which stops it from sinking in the snow. A **Powder Basket** has a larger diameter and is a godsend off-piste in soft snow.

Binding – The device that clips your boots on to your ski or snowboard. **Ski Touring** bindings release at the heel to make walking easier. In case of a fall, ski bindings allow the ski to come off to prevent injury, while snowboard bindings do not.

Bluebird – Sunny, cloudless days, often following snow overnight.

Brain Bucket – A helmet. Helmets are usually compulsory for children, but a matter of personal choice for adults in most resorts. We elected to wear helmets when our G.P.S clocked us travelling at an average of 40mph and a top speed of 60.2mph on skis. You may feel that a woolly bobble hat offers sufficient skull protection against impact with rocks, trees or other people wearing brain buckets at such velocity. It also stops people from cracking you on the nut by pulling down the safety guard on the chair lift before you're ready.

Bumps – Also known as **Moguls**. These are lumps carved into the snow, usually by skiers turning. They can be hard, soft, petite or the size of a V.W. Beetle. Now that I know how to ski them, I concede that they have a point.

Button Lift – A type of drag or cable tow ski lift which pulls a single skier uphill. It is so called because it has a circle or button on the end, which you place between your legs. Also known as a **Poma Lift** after the French manufacturing company *Poma-*

galski. There are no drag lifts in Monte Rosa. This is a shame, since they are by far the most entertaining form of lift. They pose problems for beginners and snowboarders – and the initial tug from some of them is powerful enough to launch even advanced skiers face first into the snow pack, in full view of the queue.

C

Cable Car – The largest ski lifts, which look like airborne buses or trams. They can carry a hundred or so standing passengers and are popular locations for vertiginous fight scenes, such as in the Bond film *Moonraker*.

Camber – The shape of a traditional ski, which will rest on its **Tip** and **Tail** while the midsection is a concave, upward arc. Camber makes the ski springy, which aids grip and helps it turn easily.

Carving – Turning by using the sharp **Edges** of skis or a snowboard.

Carving Ski – Narrow, waisted skis designed to perform short, clean turns on piste. See also **Parabolic**, **Shaped** or **Waisted Ski**.

Chatter – Vibration of skis at high speeds or when too much pressure is applied to the ski. This reduces contact with the snow and so, affects control.

Cornice – An overhanging ridge of wind-blown snow on the edge of a precipice. Cornices are dangerous, since they can break off unexpectedly, so don't stand either on or underneath one. Note that they can be difficult to spot from the top of a ridge or in poor visibility.

Couloir – The French word for 'corridor' – a steep, narrow chute on a mountain, often bounded by rocky cliffs.

Crampons – Spiked attachments that fit on climbing boots to give traction on ice. Ski mountaineers may use crampons to cross glaciers and ice fields or to climb on snow or ice.

Crevasse – A deep crack or fissure in an ice sheet or glacier.

Cross-Country Skiing – A type of **Nordic Skiing** or **Ski de Fond** on relatively flat ground, using narrow skis with bindings that allow the heel to release.

D

Dump – We love a big dump! A fall of fresh snow, which means... **Powder**!

E

Edge – The sharpened, metal strip on the sides of a ski or snowboard which bites into the snow to grip the slope and give control during a turn.

F

Fall Line – The most direct route down a slope, so called because if you fall, that's the direction that you will take; straight down.

First Tracks or **Fresh Tracks** – Congratulations! You are the first to ski through fresh snow.

Freeride – Similar to **Back-Country** or **Off-Piste**.

G

Goggles – Eyewear which protects your peepers from sun, glare, wind, snow and other people trying to poke you in the eye with the sharp end of their poles.

Gondola – A smaller, enclosed lift to carry approximately six to twelve passengers. Often called a bubble because it looks like one, it is the same as a French *Télécabine*.

Groomers – Groomed and prepared pistes.

Grooming – The act of snow being spread and flattened by large piste machines, or piste bashers, which bulldoze the snow and drag rakes over it to prepare it for skiers.

H

Hahnenkamm – The most demanding, World Cup downhill ski race, held annually in Kitzbühel, Austria, on a mountain with the same name.

Herringbone – Walking uphill on skis by spreading the **Tips** while keeping the **Tails** together. So called because it leaves a herringbone pattern in the snow.

Hockey Stop – The most efficient way to stop quickly; you slide your skis sideways to give the maximum resistance. The name comes from an equivalent ice hockey manoeuvre.

I

Ice Axe – A light, mountaineering axe which can be used as an anchor, to cut footholds or as a means of self-arrest to control a slide on snow. Aunty Lilian denies the latter, stating that in her experience, an ice axe provided, "an excellent mode of propulsion."

J

Ja-POW – Light, dry powder snow typical of Japan.

Jump Turn – A quick hop to release both ski edges from the ground, followed by a twist to change direction. A useful technique in steep, tight areas or to turn in thick, heavy snow.

L

Liftie – Lift Operator.

Lift Pass – The ticket that gives you access to the lift system on the mountain. It can be valid for anything from a few hours to a full season, for all or part of the ski area. These days, they are usually electronic and can indicate to the **Liftie** whether you're male, female, O.A.P or junior – or even flash up a photo, so be careful if you borrow someone's pass. If you are caught out, you can be fined and the lift pass confiscated.

M

Magic Carpet – Often found on **Nursery Slopes**, this is a conveyor belt to transport skiers and snowboarders uphill.

Moguls – **Bumps** that get carved into the snow,

usually by skiers turning, although they can be man-made for competition purposes. Mogully is the child star of *The Jungle Book*.

N

No-Fall Zone – An area where a fall is likely to result in serious injury or death.

Nordic Skiing – Usually used interchangeably with **Cross-Country Skiing**, although technically it encompasses to any type of skiing in which the heel releases from the binding. It includes **Telemark** skiing and ski jumping.

O

Off-Piste – Similar to **Back-Country** or **Freeride**. Any area off the ski slopes which is not marked, groomed, patrolled or protected against avalanche dangers is off-piste. This includes the side of the piste.

Out-of-bounds – **Off-Piste**.

P

Parabolic Skis – Modern skis are wider at the tips and tails and narrower at the waist, which makes them easier to turn, since the shape initiates a curve. The same as **Carving**, **Shaped** or **Waisted Skis**, which I will define more stupidly later.

Parallel Turn – A turn in which the skis remain alongside each other and are simply rolled on to their edges to initiate the turn.

Piste – The French word for 'trail', which is now

synonymous with a prepared slope for snowsports. (*Pista* in Italian.)

Pisteur – A person who prepares or **Grooms** the snow on the **Piste**.

Pit-Zips – Zips under the armpits which can be opened to allow ventilation.

Poling – Pushing yourself along on flat terrain using your ski poles.

Poma Lift – See **Button Lift**.

Powder Basket – See **Basket**.

Powder Gaiter – A piece of material inside the lower leg section of a pair of **Salopettes**, which is elasticated to prevent the ingress of snow.

Powder Skirt – A piece of material on the inside of a ski jacket which fastens around the waist. Like the **Powder Gaiter**, it is elasticated to keep out snow.

Powder Skis – Wide skis that float on top of fresh powder.

Powder Tracers – Lengths of brightly coloured ribbon which attach to your ski **Binding** via a loop or small karabiner, while the loose end is packed into the powder gaiter of your **Salopettes**. If your ski releases in deep snow, the ribbon lying on the surface enables you to find it easily.

Probe (Avalanche Probe) – A telescopic pole which a searcher pokes through avalanche debris to find a buried victim.

R

Rocker – Or **Reverse Camber** is a design feature of

off-piste skis appropriated from watersports. When the **Tips** and **Tails** of a ski are turned upwards, or rockered, it helps the ski to float over a surface like a water ski. The ski will usually still be **Cambered** underfoot.

S

Saisonnaires or **Saisonnières** – The seasonal workers who slave away to make your ski holiday enjoyable. It's not all sex and drugs and rock 'n' roll, although it is a bit.

Salopettes – Trousers designed for snow sports, traditionally with a high waist, possibly a bib and braces. Like wetsuits, they share the uncanny ability to shrink between seasons.

Schuss – A straight downhill ski run; or the act of making a straight downhill run on skis without turning.

Self-Arrest – A technique to stop a slide on a snowy or icy slope. It is worth learning even for piste skiing, since the barriers provided on some precipices may simply be a length of ticker tape.

Servicing – A black art, which involves repairing the bases of your skis; applying a thin layer, a few molecules thick, of the correct type of wax for the conditions; sharpening part of your **Edges** at the correct angle for your ability and the type of skiing that you wish to do – and blunting another part of them for the same reasons. That's why we entrust this to expert skiers like Carlos, Ezio and Simone in *Ambaradanspitz*.

Shaped Skis – As opposed to straight skis. A

brachiosaurus is thin at one end, thicker in the middle, and thin at the other end. Shaped skis are the opposite of a brachiosaurus. See **Carving Skis, Parabolic Skis** or **Waisted Skis.**

Shovel (Avalanche Shovel) – Used to dig out a buried victim.

Shovel – The front end of a ski, which often widens to prevent it from sinking into the snow.

Sidecut – The difference between the widest and narrowest point of a ski or snowboard. More sidecut means a shorter and sharper **Turning Radius.**

Side Slip – Sliding sideways down a slope with your skis flat on the snow and orientated ninety degrees to the **Fall Line**. A basic technique which is often neglected; a controlled side slip is an excellent skill to have up your sleeve to lose height on steep, icy slopes or places where you can't turn.

Side Step – Stepping uphill by digging the upper ski **Edges** into the snow with the skis sideways across the slope.

Ski de Fond – **Cross-Country Skiing.**

Ski Patrol – Professionally trained skiers and snowboarders employed by the resort, who are responsible for slope safety. Unlike the unpatrolled **Off-Piste**, patrolled slopes are checked and swept of stragglers at the end of the day.

Skier's Left – A dependable way of describing direction, which cannot be misinterpreted. Indicating that something is left or right depends on which way you are facing. Skier's left is the area to the left of a person travelling downhill.

Ski Mountaineering or **SkiMo** – Ascending mountains either on skis or carrying skis in order to find good snow or new, **Off-Piste** routes to ski down. **Ski Touring** involves a lot of this. **Touring Bindings** release at the heel to make walking easier.

Ski Touring – Skiing across open country, going uphill using **Skins**, as well as downhill.

Skier's Right – The area to the right of a person going downhill.

Skins – Strips of synthetic material or mohair that affix temporarily to the base of skis to facilitate climbing uphill without slipping backwards. Used in **Ski Touring** and **Ski Mountaineering**.

Skin Up – Not what you think! A sport for very thin people, clad in *Lycra,* who ascend mountains under their own steam, using **Skins**.

Snow Line – The boundary on a mountain between the snow-free and snow-covered area.

Snowplough – A skiing, braking or turning technique used by beginners. The skis are splayed in a wedge shape with the **Tips** together and **Tails** apart and the skis slightly on their inner **Edges**.

Stem Turn or **Step Turn** – Another oft' neglected basic skill. A stem turn is a halfway house between a **Snowplough** and a **Parallel Turn**. The back of the downhill ski is pushed outwards to initiate the turn and the other ski lifted or stepped to bring it parallel towards the end of the turn. A useful tool in tight spaces.

T

Tail – The rear of a ski.

T-Bar Lift – A drag or cable-tow lift where instead of a button for a single skier, there is a cross piece, which can accommodate two skiers, one on either side of the tow cable. It is essential that the two skiers are of similar height. We discovered this because, at 6'6" (2m) tall, Mark's knees are at the same height as my bum, which did not make for a comfortable ride.

Telemark Skiing – Named after the Telemark region in Norway, where it originated. The Telemark ski **Binding** fixes only the toe to the ski, leaving the heel free. Turns are initiated by moving one knee down in a deep lunge.

Tip – The front of a ski.

Touring Bindings – Ski Bindings that release at the heel to allow the skier to walk or **Skin**.

Transceiver – See **Avalanche Beacon**.

Traverse – Crossing a slope or the side of a mountain.

Turning Radius – The natural circle made by a ski or a snowboard when placed on its **Edge**. More **Sidecut** means a tighter turning radius.

Twin Tip – Skis turned up at both the tail and tip. Twin tips make skiing backwards easier, which is good for tricks and showing off.

V

Vertical Drop – The distance between the highest point of a mountain or ski run and its lowest point.

W

Waisted Skis – skis that see the snow for only one week every winter. Kidding. **See Carving, Parabolic** or **Shaped Skis.**

Whiteout – When visibility drops to zero or almost zero due to cloud, mist, heavy snow or all three.

APPENDIX 1

Ten Tips to Keep Chilly Canines Cosy!

Invaluable advice for taking furry friends to cooler climes

When we took our precious pups skiing with us, we found it very difficult to find *any* information *at all* about the hazards of taking small dogs into a cold climate. In case you are considering taking your own Pups On Piste, or the U.K. is expecting to be crippled by a few millimetres of the wrong kind of snow, here are our top tips.

Some dogs, like Huskies, were bred for cold climates and have a double coat. A waterproof outer coat covers a downy insulation layer. It is also obvious that large dogs will manage better in colder temperatures, because of their greater body mass.

The main cold-weather hazards to look out for with all types of dogs are as follows;

1. Cold

Small dogs have little body mass to retain heat – but they do have a large surface area over which to lose it, so they can get very cold, very quickly.

Our Cavapoos have soft, long coats. They were bred to feel nice to cuddle and stroke – not provide the best insulation or water resistance in Arctic temperatures.

The Fab Four are good at telling us that they are too cold – they cry and ask to be picked up. If your dog starts shivering, whining, trying to burrow or if he stops playing and becomes lethargic, he is probably too cold. As a rule of thumb, if it is too cold for you, it is too cold for your dog.

I am no advocate of doggie clothing for fashion, but for winter, a doggie jumper provides two benefits – an additional layer of insulation and coverage to prevent snow from balling up in long fur. Most of the dog coats we bought didn't work; snow got inside the coat and they did not cover the belly adequately.

After much research, we bought *Equafleece Polartec™ fleece dog jumpers* and can't speak too highly of them. The jumpers fit closely and cover most of the dog, preventing snow from balling up on all but the lower legs, lower belly and backside (which have to remain uncovered to allow for calls of nature!) They insulate well and dry snow shakes off them, although if they do get wet, *Polartec™* wicks moisture away from the dog and will still keep him warm.

As with humans, dogs can suffer from

Hypothermia and Frostbite. *(see footnote to recognise the signs.)* Even if your furry friends are wearing coats, monitor their ears, paws, tails and noses, which are still exposed to the cold.

2. Winter Toxins

In winter, humans spread salt and antifreeze around a lot. Both can be toxic to pets. Anti-freeze (ethylene glycol) tastes sweet but is poisonous to dogs in tiny quantities. Ingesting too much salt can cause dehydration and lead to organ failure. To safeguard against toxins being taken in when licking paws, rinse your tail-wagger's tums and tootsies after your walk and don't allow them to drink from puddles or slush near roads.

3. Snow Removal

If snow balls up in your dog's fur, it needs to be removed as soon as you get back indoors. We found the easiest way was to soak it off in a lukewarm bath or shower before a thorough drying. Only a fully dry doggie should be allowed back out into the cold.

4. DON'T LEAVE DOGS IN CARS. EVER!

Cold cars are just as dangerous for dogs as hot cars in the summer. Don't leave your dog freezing to death in a cold car!

5. Safety and Security

Beware what lies beneath – when out walking,

keep everyone close to make sure your fur babies don't do a disappearing act through an unsafe surface like a frozen lake or pond, which could be concealed under snow.

Our Rosie is a real escape artist – so snow piled up near a boundary fence would be too much of a temptation to escape to freedom. As it melts, heavy snow can slide off roofs and cause injury to dogs (and people!) – so beware what lies above as well.

You might feel safe from avalanches in the U.K., but Britain's most deadly avalanche happened in Lewes, East Sussex – not too far from England's sunny South Coast!

6. Always Walk on the Sunny Side of the Street!
If it is freezing, try to walk during warmer periods of the day or when the sun is shining. We found that a few shorter walks or a walk and a play session were better than one long walk in freezing temperatures.

7. Alive & Well & Livin' In…
Don't leave pets outside in winter weather. Indoors, make sure they have a cosy bed, not a cold, draughty floor to snuggle on. Our dogs are like heat-seeking missiles – so we make sure that they can't burn themselves if they cuddle up to radiators, heaters or log fires.

8. Hydration
If you're a fan of Intrepid Adventurer Bear Grylls,

you will know that cold and altitude are very dehydrating – and it is impossible to eat enough snow to rehydrate.

The same applies to dogs, so remember to take water even when you're walking in winter. Indoors, extra heating might cause dehydration, so as ever, make sure that plenty of clean, fresh water is always available.

9. Winter Feeding

If you don't want a pooch with a paunch, make sure that their insulation comes from fur or their cosy winter jackets – not an unhealthy layer of fat.

Indoor dogs don't need more energy to keep warm. In fact, if you are doing shorter walks, your pup may actually need less food in winter, so adjust quantities accordingly.

10. Winter Grooming Tips

It was not just because we were in Italy that The Fab Four needed to look their best. Grooming is actually a very important winter survival tip.

A. Fur

A clean, well-groomed coat keeps your dog insulated. Although we rinsed the dogs frequently after walks, we rarely used shampoo. Shampoo can strip out the natural oils in the coat, which help to keep your pup warm. We made sure that everyone was dried thoroughly, especially before they went back outside.

A longer coat will provide more warmth. We found that a trim around the legs minimised clinging ice balls and helped to prevent matting under the doggie jumpers.

B. Itchy Skin

We didn't have any problems with dry, flaky skin. If you do, you could consider adding a skin and coat supplement to your dog's food, such as coconut oil or fish oil. A humidifier (technical term for a bowl of water near a radiator!) may also help since cold, altitude and central heating can be very drying.

C. Paw Care

These are the precautions that we took to keep our dogs' paws in tip top winter condition;

1. **Trim nails** – this stops splaying, which helps to prevent accumulation of snow and ice between pads and improves traction.
2. **Trim fur between pads** and around feet to prevent accumulation of snow balls in the fur.
3. **Paw Balm** – protects pads from salt and chemical de-icers. We applied *Musher's Secret* every couple of days. It was brilliant at reducing snow accumulation and kept the pads moisturised. It also works on leather hiking boots and ski gloves!
4. **Wash & dry paws and tums** after each walk

to remove toxic, drying and stinging ice, salt and chemicals. Check for cracks in the pads or any redness between the toes.
5. **During the Walk** – check and remove any ice balls which form between pads. Take a rag or towel to wipe salt off paws on longer walks.
6. **Boots** – we agonised over boots. Much of the advice that we read said that dogs' paws are adapted to cope with different temperatures, so boots are not necessary. And they don't stay on. As reported, we tried some boots. They did not stay on. They also caused the pups to slip when wearing them, so we gave up.

We took all of the above advice with their paws and when it was really cold, we did shorter walks at warmer times of day. In a three-month season, we didn't have so much as a cracked pad.

Take care, stay safe but most of all – ENJOY THE SNOW!

Footnote

Hypothermia

Dogs must keep their core body temperature higher than humans – between 38.3 and 39.2°C, compared to 36.5 - 37.5°C for humans.

Hypothermia happens when the core temperature of the body starts to drop. For a dog, severe hypothermia occurs if the core temperature drops below 28°C. Hypothermia is a serious condition and can be fatal, so consult a vet if you're in any doubt.

Hypothermia is caused by spending too long in the cold, getting wet in the cold, especially if it is windy, or if a dog with poor health or circulation is exposed to the cold.

Initial symptoms are shivering, cold feet and ears leading to lethargy and signs of depression. Slow heartbeat and slow breathing, dilated pupils and a lack of response to stimuli could indicate severe hypothermia.

To treat mild hypothermia, wrap your dog in warmed blankets (heat them on a radiator, in a tumble dryer or with a hairdryer) and / or place a hot water bottle in a towel on his tummy (careful not to burn the skin). This will help to return his body temperature to normal.

If your dog is suffering from hypothermia due to the cold, he may also have signs of frostbite;

Frostbite

Frostbite happens when blood is pulled from extremities back to the core to keep warm. Ice crystals then form in the tissues, which rupture and kill the cells.

Ears, paws and tails are particularly vulnerable, since they are not protected by even the best doggie coats.

Like sunburn, frostbite is not usually obvious immediately. Signs to look out for are the skin turning pale or bluish-grey, or it may go hard and cold. As frostbitten areas warm up and the blood returns, they can be very painful. Severely frostbitten flesh eventually turns black and sloughs off.

Treatment for minor frostbite is similar to Hypothermia; slowly warm the affected areas, but do not squeeze or rub them or use direct heat. Consult your vet.

Both of these conditions are easily preventable if you follow my advice on keeping chilly canines cosy!

APPENDIX 2

Tips for Winter Walkies in Monte Rosa & Other Ski Areas

Monte Rosa takes pride in being Dog Friendly. That said, we could find NO information whatsoever on how and where to walk dogs before we arrived. Of course, once in resort, we sussed it out ourselves and it was actually very straightforward.

Here are my Top Tips on winter walking. Route advice is specific to the Gressoney Valley, but the more general tips apply in other resorts.

Dog Friendly access to the Mountains

Dogs can visit many mountain huts and travel on shuttle buses, gondolas and cable cars. Although it is not always enforced, dogs should be muzzled on buses and cable cars. If you don't carry a muzzle, be prepared to be refused entry occasionally. *Gordon's Irish Pub* and the *Da Giovanni* bar and restaurant in Staffal are both dog friendly. There are dog-friendly pubs and restaurants in Gressoney la Trinité and Gressoney St Jean.

Where to Go for Winter Walkies

There are plenty of well-marked and pisted skinning tracks, snow-shoe trails and Nordic skiing pistes *(Ski de Fond)* which are ideal for winter walkies. These Nordic tracks can be found in most of the resort villages and the skinning tracks in the mountains are marked with green piste markers. We have seen dogs bounding down the edge of the slope with their owners, but for safety, Paws on Piste is strictly forbidden in most resorts.

Marked tracks are generally relatively safe and avalanche protected. Some of the huge network of summer walking paths may be accessible for winter walking depending on conditions, but take heed of local advice, since they may not be safe.

What to Wear for Winter Walkies

Humans

Snow shoes can be hired, but are only necessary if you are trekking across deep or melting spring snow (which would not be suitable for our small dogs.) On the pisted tracks, we simply wear hiking boots fitted with *YakTrax* snow-chains-for-shoes to give extra grip. We didn't even need gaiters. Walking poles may be helpful on some of the steeper and less groomed terrain, although the poles sink in deep snow, unless fitted with a powder basket.

Take layers of warm, thermal clothing. On sunny days, we find soft-shell trousers adequate. Don't forget snacks, water for you and pups and a mobile phone programmed with the emergency number.

Doggies

Appendix 1; 'Ten Tips to Keep Chilly Canines Cosy' covers the rudiments of care for wintery woofers.

The Hazards of Winter Walkies

Winter Walkies are prone to the same hazards as off-piste skiing, so check locally where is safe to walk.

- Keep an eye on the weather. Even if tracks are well marked, it is easy to become disorientated in poor visibility.
- Make sure that you are properly equipped and speak to the Mountain Guides and / or Tourist Information regarding where is safe to walk.

The conditions can vary enormously; as I mentioned, in our second season, we were shocked to find several of our regular walks from the previous year buried under enormous avalanches.

Dog Sitter Not Required!

Sylvia looked after the pups the week we were on

our course, but mostly, we found a dog sitter unnecessary. One of the advantages of our location in Staffal, right in the centre of Monte Rosa's compact ski area, is that it is really quick and easy to get back for lunch and check on your doggies.

Since we had the whole season, we did not feel compelled stay out for full days. We tended to ski in the morning and walk the dogs in the afternoon, when it was warmer. Winter walkies added a wonderful dimension to our ski holiday. Another way to enjoy the snowy landscape – and great for stretching those skiing muscles. The surprising benefit of walking in the ski resort was that, in part, it also satisfied my craving to get into the back-country – and helped with route-finding off-piste.

In Conclusion

We found that taking our pups skiing with us very uncomplicated. There were plenty of places that were safe and easy to walk – and our Fur Babies absolutely loved the snow!

ACKNOWLEDGMENTS

I would like to thank the following people;

Phil Smith – and all the instructors and guides at *Snoworks*, www.snoworks.com, for wonderful, backcountry adventures and for improving our skiing so markedly.

Debbie Purse – at *Book Covers for You* for once again coming up trumps with a cover that is a work of genius.

www.bookcoversforyou.com

Caroline Smith – for her wonderful friendship, services as a Grammar Nazi Extraordinaire and patient beta reading of my manuscript.

Sophie Wallace – @SophieWallaceProofreading for support and advice beyond the call of duty, as well as ever perfect and painstaking proofing.

Elisabetta and **Matilde** – the wonderful vets in Pont St Martin, who have given such wonderful care to

Oscar and The Fab Four in our first and successive ski seasons.

To My Readers Around the World – as authors, we bare our souls for your entertainment. Your kind words, reviews and encouragement mean so much.

And of course, Mark, Kai, Rosie, Ruby and Lani for filling every day with unconditional love and joy.

(Please note that I have no connection with any companies mentioned here, other than as a satisfied client. I paid for all services and receive no incentives.)

And Finally – A Request

I aim to entertain and inform – and hopefully inspire. If I got close, I would be unbelievably grateful if you could leave a review on Amazon, Goodreads or anywhere else.

No essays required. Even a single sentence is greatly appreciated.

And if you could spread the word, tell your friends or share us on Facebook, The Fab Four and I will be eternally grateful.

Dog Bless You All

ABOUT THE AUTHOR

The Author in front of Gabiet and the Moos Valley with Lani, Kai, Rosie and Ruby

"Why can't you just get a nice dress like all the other girls?"

I was wondering what to say about myself. One guide on *How to Write an Author Biog.* suggested the following steps:

1. A Punchy, Impactful First Sentence.

The above was what my Mum said when I bought a gum shield and a pair of sparring mitts with the birthday money she gave me. Like my aunts, I have always found doing stuff, like karate, climbing trees or riding horses and bikes, far more rewarding than painting my nails.

Perhaps this also explains why my brother would solicit and then promptly dismiss my advice regarding the fairer sex, using the justification that, "You're not a proper woman."

2. Introduce Your Authority Area

I wrote my first travel memoir aged 14. *The Road Goes Ever On* described a five-day tour on horseback around the ancient pack pony routes of Britain's Lake District. It came second in a national competition, open to all ages.

My urge to write is as compelling as my desire to travel. I won't mention the high points of my literary career, such as having an article on the recycling rates of London Underground trains published in the snappily-titled magazine, *Local Authority Waste and Environment.* (And yes, this august publication *has* appeared on *Have I Got News for You*!)

I have obsessively kept diaries of my adventures on six of the seven continents, including a year of 'Maternity Leave' given by a confused boss,

"But Jackie – you don't even have a boyfriend!"

"I know. I don't want to go through all that messy business of childbirth. I just want to travel around the world, then have my job back when I return."

Since giving up work forever to embark on our full-time Continental Drift, I set up my blog, *World Wide*

Walkies. My aim is not only to entertain; I want to share what we have learned and show that if you are prepared to compromise and make brave choices, it is achievable to live the life you want.

Then, a few people said, "You should write a book!" So, I did.

In fact, being a compulsive scribbler, I wrote a few. *Pups on Piste* is number four.

3. Build Credibility Without Overly Bragging.

All of my books have five-star reviews on Amazon and Goodreads. *Dog on the Rhine* teeters in and out of the *Amazon* Bestseller list for 'Rhine' and 'German Travel'. On my 20th Wedding Anniversary, I received a surprise invitation to a gala dinner in Bucharest because *Dogs 'n' Dracula* was a finalist in the Romania Insider Awards. Both Prince Charles, who has personal connections with Romania, and The British Ambassador to Romania now own a copy.

Name-dropping the heir to the throne of the United Kingdom – that's not overly bragging, is it?

4. Add A Personal Touch

So far this season, I can't fit into my pink salopettes. I chose pink in an attempt to be a proper woman.

@JacquelineLambertAuthor
www.WorldWideWalkies.com

www.ingramcontent.com/pod-product-compliance
Lightning Source LLC
Chambersburg PA
CBHW060520080526
44586CB00012B/554